Ideas and Institutions in Indian Political Thought

[Based on the directivs of NEP]

Foreword by Prof. Rekha Saxena
Head, Department of Political Science
University of Delhi

SHUBHRA PARMAR
Assistant Professor
Department of Political Science
Bhagini Nivedita College
University of Delhi, New Delhi

TANNI MOITRA
Assistant Professor
Department of History
Sharda School of Humanities & Social Sciences
Sharda University, Greater Noida

PHI Learning Private Limited
Delhi-110092
2026

*In fond memory of **Shri Asoke K. Ghosh** (October 1942 – February 2024), Founder Chairman and Managing Director of PHI Learning, whose vision endlessly inspires.*

The Legacy Continues. . . .

Published by Pushpita Ghosh, PHI Learning Private Limited, Rimjhim House, 111, Patparganj Industrial Estate, Delhi-110092 and Printed by Multi Colour Services, 92, DSIDC Sheds, Okhla Industrial Area, Phase-I, New Delhi-110020.

₹475.00

IDEAS AND INSTITUTIONS IN INDIAN POLITICAL THOUGHT
Shubhra Parmar and Tanni Moitra

ISBN-978-93-5443-927-8 (Print Book)
ISBN-978-93-5443-982-7 (e-Book)

Contents

Foreword

Recent scholarship and research on ancient Indian politics and statecraft has highlighted several significant dimensions of ancient Indian politics. The introduction of the paper "Ideas and Institutions in Indian Political Thought" is a much applauded effort to break down the eurocentrism of Political Science in Indian academics. It will make the students aware about their own cultural roots. It is good to study political systems, thoughts and traditions of other countries but that should not be at the cost of ignorance of one's own political traditions and thoughts.

There is a need amongst the students to break down the inferiority complex of their own traditions and thoughts in comparison to Western traditions and thoughts. Many of the ideas attributed to Western modernity such as democracy, republics, federalism, etc. can be traced to the ancient Indian roots. Therefore, the course will make the students culturally aware and make their knowledge historically situated rather than abstract knowledge.

I congratulate the authors of the book for taking this initiate to write a textbook on this paper. There is surely a dearth of books on ancient Indian political institutions and this book will be a great help for students. The book is comprehensive and covers all the topics of the syllabus. Moreover, it is written in lucid language making it easier for students to understand the complex concepts in simple language. I am sure this would motivate other scholars to work on this under explored area.

Prof. Rekha Saxena
Head, Department of Political Science
University of Delhi

विभागाध्यक्ष/Head
राजनीति विज्ञान विभाग
Department of Political Science
दिल्ली विश्वविद्यालय / University of Delhi
दिल्ली-110007 / Delhi-110007

Preface

We are happy to introduce a textbook on 'Ideas and Institutions in Indian Political Thought' for the students of Political Science. This paper is introduced for the first time by the University of Delhi to the students of BA (Hons.) Political Science as a Discipline Specific Core, based on UGCF 2022–NEP 2020.

We hope the students and teachers will find this text valuable for them. Any constructive feedback is welcomed from the readers to improve this text in the future edition.

Acknowledgements

We would like to express our deep gratitude and heartfelt special thanks to Professor Rekha Saxena, Head of the Political Science Department at University of Delhi, for her academic excellence, invaluable mentorship, support and motivation. We appreciate her support and confidence that she has shown in our abilities.

The first author would especially like to thank Principal Professor Raj Bhardwaj of Bhagini Nivedita College for her unwavering encouragement and motivation. The author would also like to express her gratitude to Dr. Punam Dagar, Head, Department of Political Science, Bhagini Nivedita College. Also, she would like to thank Professor Aloka Dutta and Professor Nirmala Rana for their encouragement and inspiration.

The second author would like to thank the Dean of Sharda School of Humanities and Social Sciences (SSHSS), Prof. Anviti Gupta for her encouragement. The author is also grateful to her colleagues, Dr. Khushboo Kumari and Dr. Shradha, Department of History, SSHSS, for supporting an interdisciplinary work intersecting Political Science and History.

We would like to extend our sincere gratitude to the entire team of PHI Learning Private Limited, especially to Ms. Pallavi Ghosh, Brand Strategist at PHI Learning and Ms. Babita Misra, Publishing Editor, for their unwavering support and patience while we wrote the book. We owe a tremendous debt of gratitude to our colleagues, who helped us in every way. The authors are also incredibly appreciative of their devoted parents, sister, brother, daughter, and spouse who had incredible and unshakable faith in their talents. Their constant support allowed us to complete this assignment. We are appreciative to our friends, colleagues, and fellow faculty at Bhagini Nivedita College and Sharda University for their inspiration. Finally, but just as importantly, we want to thank all of our wonderful students for their insightful remarks and recommendations.

Shubhra Parmar, Ph.D.
Tanni Moitra, Ph.D.

1

Statecraft in Ancient India

1.1 UNDERSTANDING STATE AND NATION

In December 1933 a treaty known as the Montevideo Convention on the Rights and Duties of States was signed at the Seventh International Convention of American States. The significance of the Convention was that it gave a modern and internationally accepted theoretical approach to define the 'state'. One of its most frequently referred sections is Article 1 which sets out the conditions required by an entity to qualify as a state. It states :

'The state as a person of international law should possess the following qualifications:

(a) a permanent population;
(b) a defined territory;
(c) government; and
(d) capacity to enter into relations with the other states.'[1]

Article 1, Montevideo Convention

It is important to note that statehood, ever since the early 20th century, is fundamentally a subject regulated by international law. John Dunn rightly remarks that the Modern State is 'the principal institutional site of political experience'.[2] According to Miller's description, the State is the primary focus of international relations.[3] Before World War II only 75 states had existed and by 2005 there were almost 200.[4] Today, we are therefore most

1 Original text: https://treaties.un.org/doc/Publication/UNTS/LON/Volume%20165/v165.pdf
2 John Dunn, *The Cunning of Unreason*, Harper Collins, New York, 2000, p. 66.
3 J.D.B. Miller, *A World of States*, Croom Helm, London, 1981.
4 J. Crawford, *The Creation of States in International Law*, 2nd edition, Claredon Press,

accustomed to modern understanding of State; however, it is worth noting that our present existence within the framework of Modern State has evolved and undergone changes through centuries. Historically, we have witnessed various institutional forms of 'political experience'.

Niccolo Machiavelli (1469–1527), the Italian political theorist who is known for his famous political treatise ***The Prince,*** is credited with the first use of the term "state" in the 16th century. In the opening of the treatise, Machiavelli employs the term "state" (***stato*** in Italian, meaning "status") in a neutral sense to encompass to cover "all forms of organization of supreme political power, whether republican or princely". For Machiavelli the State led by and created by a strong and powerful Prince the State would be the tool by which the Prince will establish his rule and free Italy from the foreign powers, including the Roman Church. The state is the instrument of the Prince who will to shape the republic or principality so that it would be more effective than the forms of political rule one encountered among the various city-republics and principalities of his time.[5] Quentin Skinner has illustrated that the term began to be discussed, in the English-speaking world around this period and acquired a meaning close to the modern sense, referring to an abstract, impersonal entity, separate from the person of the prince.[6] Machiavelli's concept of the state is transmitted from Florence and to the West, to England and France and his concept was used and modified by the various statesmen and legislators who sought to use Machiavelli's concept to strengthen the political order they lived in.[7] The concept of the state was reformulated by political thinkers such as Gentili, Bodin, Grotius and Hobbes which subsequently transformed the Machiavellian notion.

The notion of state received a renewed understanding over a period of a century and got transformed in the hands of the French political philosopher Jean Bodin's (1530–1596) ***Six books of the Republic,*** published in 1576.[8] Bodin introduced and propagated the concept of sovereignty as concentrated in the hands of the sovereign, the King. Bodin's idea of a sovereign king was occasioned by a background extreme political violence and instability in France, driven by religious conflict between

---

2006, p. 4.

[5] Clifford Angell Bates, "The Trajectory of Machiavelli's Concept of State in Early Modern Politics," *Dialogi Polityczne*, November 2022, 1(32), pp. 9–10.

[6] Quentin Skinner, 'The State' in Ball, T., Farr, J. and Hanson, R. (eds.), *Political Innovation and Conceptual Change*, Cambridge University Press, Cambridge 1989, p. 326.

[7] Clifford Angell Bates, "The Trajectory of Machiavelli's Concept of State in Early Modern Politics," *Dialogi Polityczne,* November 2022, 1(32), p. 7.

[8] Richard Devetak, The Modern State, in Richard Devetak, Anthony Burke, Jim George (eds.), *An Introduction to International Relations*, Cambridge University Press, Cambridge, p. 138.

the French Protestants (Huguenots) and the Catholic Kings resulting in St Bartholomew's Day Massacre in 1572.[9] Bodin argued that power and authority should be concentrated in a single decision-maker, preferably the king and believed that a well-ordered society required an 'absolute and perpetual power', namely the sovereign, who would hold the 'highest power of command'.[10] One of the key aspects of sovereignty, as presented by the Frenchman, was that law and order could only be maintained within a society if one power alone possessed a distinct prerogative across the territorial jurisdiction.[11] Bodin contended that a powerful sovereign is required to suppress anarchy and ensure prospects of political stability.

Thomas Hobbes (1588–1679) who published ***Leviathan*** in 1651 argued for a strong central authority personified in the King and his state to enforce decisions. Hobbes's primary idea was the establishment of state sovereignty around a theory of political obligation[12] and argued that prior to the formation of state, individuals live in a 'state of nature' where there is no 'common Power to keep them all in awe'. In the absence of an overarching authority, there can be no peace or security because there is nothing to stop individuals harming one another. The state of nature is a condition lacking any rules and therefore any justice; mutual fear and insecurity are its defining features. According to Hobbes, only the establishment of a sovereign state—through a 'social contract' where the sovereign promises to protect and subjects promise to obey—can create the conditions of security and order necessary for society to develop freedom and industry.[13]

The modern notion of the state with a sovereign ruler at its centre emerged in Europe within a background of recurrent violence, civil war, religious conflict and race for weaponry. Europe was overrun by perennial warfare with as many as 112 wars being fought between 1555 to 1648. The state became practically identified as 'war machine'. There was a close connection between the building of state and organized warfare and the historical condition of Europe is famously captured in the remark of Charles Tilly in the statement 'war made the state, and the state made war'[14]. Max Weber writing in the 19th century stressed, 'what defines the state first and foremost is its 'monopoly of the legitimate use of physical force'.[15] The most essential attribute of the state was power which was

[9] *Ibid*, p. 138
[10] *Ibid*, pp. 138–139.
[11] *Ibid*, p. 139.
[12] *Ibid*, p. 139.
[13] *Ibid*, p. 139.
[14] Charles Tilly, Charles, 'Reflections on the History of European state-making' in Tilly, C. (ed.), *The formation of National States in Europe*, Princeton University Press, Princeton, 1975, p. 42.
[15] René Grotenhuis, *Nation-Building as Necessary Effort in Fragile States*, Amsterdam University Press, 2016, p. 33.

manifested through its function of enforcing law that it is a body of rules which has behind it an organized power acknowledged to have the right of coercion as against recalcitrant individuals. From this point of view the fundamental political relation is that of sovereign and subject.[16]

It is important to note at this juncture that in contrast to the modern and pre-modern State, Medieval Europe (c. 500–1500 CE) presented a distinct political structure different from the Machiavellian conception of state. Europe in the medieval period was rather decentralized and shared among different actors—not just the prince, but also the Pope, the Holy Roman Emperor, and Dukes and Counts, many of whom were related by blood. Quite often territory was partitioned, splintered, non-contiguous, and there existed no effective centre or capital capable of exerting its will exclusively and effectively over its disparate territories.[17] This decentralized political structure is identified as Medieval Feudalism often characterized by the fragmentation of political power, public power in private possession, and armed forces secured through private agreements.[18] The King lacked both administrative and financial capacity to extend his authority across divided kingdom and would appoint representatives, usually a count or duke, to administer justice at the local levels. The local counts exercised 'full military, judicial and financial power' at the king's behest.[19] The counts and dukes consolidated their power by fighting wars, administering law and justice, and raising revenue through taxation, they became increasingly proprietorial. 'They became virtually independent rulers'.[20] Overtime, the local power bases of counts and dukes grew to the point where they could challenge the capacity of royal power to impose its will.

Unlike the State which has a more or less accepted definition, 'nation' as a concept does not have a generally accepted definition. Nation and the state are not same thing but share several components. Anthony D. Smith describes a nation as 'a named human population sharing a historic territory, common myths and historical memories, a mass, public culture, a common economy and common legal rights and duties for all members'.[21] Benedict Anderson defines nation as 'an imagined political community—and imagined as both inherently limited and sovereign'.[22] The nation is about identity, who we are in the sense of 'self-identification'. The nation has to do with something subjective, even if it is a collective subjectivity, distinct from the objective features of states. This is not just adding a new

---

[16] George H. Sabine, "The Concept of the State as Power," *The Philosophical Review*, Jul., 1920, Vol. 29, No. 4 (Jul., 1920), p. 302.
[17] *Ibid*, p. 137.
[18] *Ibid*, p. 137.
[19] Joseph Strayer, *Feudalism*, Van Nostrand, Princeton 1965, p. 30.
[20] *Ibid*, p. 30.
[21] Anthony D. Smith, *National Identity*, Penguin, London, 1991, p. 43.
[22] Benedict Anderson, *Imagined Community*, Verso, New York, 1983, p. 6.

element, but fundamentally changing the notion of 'nation' compared to the notion of 'state': The state is about institutions, structures and systems, the nation is about identity; the state is about a collective objectivity, the nation is about a collective subjectivity.[23] The construction of national identity is therefore a process of selection, bringing together those elements that fit well together to create an identity people can and wish to identify with and leaving out elements that could disturb a coherent picture. The efforts to trace back the nation into history, to link the existing nation to its historical roots, are deliberate actions to underpin a national identity of an actual living community with historical events, persons and narratives.[24] Hence, the state and the nation are inextricably intertwined and a legitimate relationship may not be established between the ruler and the subject without active affirmation and a sense of togetherness as envisioned through the idea of Nation-State.

1.2 UNDERSTANDING STATECRAFT

The term "statecraft" is commonly defined as the 'art of conducting state affairs'.[25] It incorporates the development of strategies for national interest for the purpose of running the state and encompasses all the domains within the jurisdiction of the state like domestic and foreign affairs, diplomacy and administration. Statecraft is a significant aspect of the state as it ensures its existence, continuity, survival and success through the policies framed.

In order to understand statecraft, it is essential to distinguish it from political theory and political philosophy which form the other areas of intellectual exercise within the domain of political science. Political theory reflects upon political phenomenon, processes and institutions and on actual political behavior by subjecting it to philosophical or ethical criterion. It considers the question of the best political order, which is a part of a larger and a more fundamental question; namely, the ideal form of life that a human being ought to lead within a larger community. Political philosophy on the other hand provides general answers to questions such as what is justice and deals with various other concept; also the distinction between 'is' and 'ought' and the larger issues of politics. Political philosophy is a part of normative political theory, for it attempts to establish inter-relationships between concepts. A third form of political thought comprising of political testaments, didactic political writings and political advice may be identified as the theory of statecraft.

---

[23] René Grotenhuis, *Nation-Building as Necessary Effort in Fragile States*, Amsterdam University Press, 2016, p. 28.

[24] *Ibid*, p. 29.

[25] Statecraft Definition and Meaning—Merriam-Webster.

The history of statecraft may be traced back to ancient Greece; just like the origins of political theory may be traced to Plato, the theory of statecraft may be traced to his contemporary Isocrates. Isocrates (436–338 BC) was an ancient Greek rhetorician famous for his oratory[26] skills and speeches composed and delivered as political advice to the Greek rulers. In one of his major orations titled ***Philippus*** in the year 346 Isocrates wrote his discourse which he sent to Philip II of Macedon urging him to lead the Hellenic cities in an invasion of Persia by assuming a joint leadership with Sparta in a war against Persia.[27] He is said to have remarked that he hopes to persuade both his fellow citizens and Philip that reconciliation of the Hellenic cities and an expedition against the Persians under the leadership of the Macedonian king would be to their advantage. Similarly, two of his major discourses, ***Ad Nicoclem*** and ***Nicocles,*** were directed to Nicocles who was praised for his benevolent and successful rule which was achieved by replenishing the treasury without being oppressive to his subjects through exorbitant taxes. Ancient Greece is well known for schooling rulers in the art of managing the state and molding political behavior. In his famous work ***Republic,*** Plato describes his failed attempt to transform Dionysus of Syracuse from a tyrant to a philosopher king through his political philosophy.[28] After his unsuccessful effort, he turned to founding his ***Academy*** for training and making future leaders. John E. Tashjean remarks in this context that the strategy of the ***Academy*** was to catch the political leader before he became a man of power: the twig must be bent in time."[29]

Statecraft has a history of continuity across time period and has not remained confined to Greece. The notion flourished within a remarkable geographical extent which includes other European countries, Mesopotamia, Ancient India, China and the medieval Arab world. The ***Arthasastra*** of Kautilya and the conception of ***Rajadharma*** is the representative example of statecraft in ancient India. Similarly an entire genre of Islamic literature emerged in the medieval period known as ***Mirror for Princes. Mirror for Princes*** offers advice to a ruler or ruler-to-be, concerning the exercise of royal power and the well-being of the body-politic[30] and were meant

---

[26] In ancient Greece and Rome, oratory was studied as a component of rhetoric which was a composition and delivery of speeches, and was an important skill in public and private life.

[27] See, John E. Tashjean, "On Theory of Statecraft," *The Review of Politics*, Vol. 35, No. 3 (Jul., 1973).

[28] See, Robin Waterfield, *Plato of Athens: A Life in Philosophy*, Oxford University Press, New York, 2023.

[29] John E. Tashjean, "On Theory of Statecraft," *The Review of Politics*, Vol. 35, No. 3 (Jul., 1973), p. 379.

[30] See, Louise Marlow (ed.), *Medieval Muslim Mirrors for Princes: An Anthology of Arabic, Persian and Turkish Political Advice*, Cambridge University Press, 2023.

to be for the working of institutions. The work of Nizam al-Mulk titled ***Siyasatnama*** offers extremely valuable material on the organization and working of the court and the administrative institutions under the Great Seljuqs is the most significant example of this genre.[31] Niccolo Machiavelli's ***The Prince*** composed in the 15th century is again a classic example of statecraft. Statecraft theory continued down to the 18th century in Europe when in 1773 and 1774 Diderot gave political advice to Catherine the Great in St. Petersburg[32]

1.3 THE STATE IN ANCIENT INDIA: INTERPRETATION BY BENI PRASAD

Though it is impossible to trace the evolution of Hindu political structures, they are as old as Greek political institutions in origin. Despite the incredible developments in oriental studies over the past century, no political history of India exists before the sixth century B.C. Many kings' dates are uncertain, and it is impossible to determine the exact dates of the majority of Hindu poets, philosophers, grammarians, legal scholars, and political writers. Additionally, there is little source material available for the study of the political and practical workings of Hindu political institutions, and it is challenging to interpret administrative and fiscal terms.

A picture that is assembled from texts written hundreds or thousands of years apart might be fascinating in its whole, but it might not accurately reflect any particular era. It is also not possible to use documents from distant locations for a single area. Any document should, in general, be treated independently and linked to others only on the most reliable foundation due to the unpredictability of dates and the general obscurity of the subject. Social structure, location, racial makeup, and economic conditions all had a significant impact on how Hindu political systems functioned.[33]

While interpreting the state of ancient India, Beni Prasad examined the effects of geography, the predominance of agriculture, population, and forms of government, caste, villages, industries, and commerce, guilds, racial characteristics, the makeup of government, groups, and religion.

---

[31] C.E. Bosworth, "An Early Arabic Mirror for Princes: Tāhir Dhū l-Yamīnain's Epistle to His Son ʿAbdallāh (206/821)," *Journal of Near Eastern Studies* , Jan., 1970, Vol. 29, No. 1 (Jan., 1970), pp. 25–41.

[32] John E. Tashjean, "On Theory of Statecraft," *The Review of Politics* , Jul., 1973, Vol. 35, No. 3 (Jul., 1973), p. 378.

[33] Beni Prasad, The state in Ancient India: Study in the structure and Practical working of Political Institutions in North India in Ancient Times, The Indian Press, Allahabad, 1928, pp. 1–16.

1.4 THE HINDU THEORY OF STATE: INTERPRETATION BY BENOY KUMAR SARKAR

The Hindu thinkers tried to understand the state by differentiating it from the non-state.

1.4.1 Why do We Need a State?

Since human civilization was first essentially a tribal one, all people were believed to be equal and deserving of the same rights. Battles for control of resources and the emergence of a distinct economy—or a society organized at multiple levels—led to the emergence of the concept of the state. The concept of the Law of Fish is mentioned in the ancient Indian philosophy known as Matsya-Nyaya. According to the saying, "Big fish eat smaller fish," which implies that the strong eats the weak, this fundamental law of nature is explained. It is comparable to the 'Law of the Jungle'. Just like huge fish eat little fish during droughts, there is no ruler in a condition of chaos and the powerful eat the weak. As a result, the necessity of a ruler was seen as absolute. The administration of justice and the upkeep of law and order are the two main duties of the state, both of which are necessary to ensure the safety of its citizens and the nation as a whole.

1.4.2 The Doctrine of Matsya-Nyaya (The Logic of Fish)

Hindu scholars attempted to distinguish between the state and the non-state in order to comprehend the state. They approached it by rationally distinguishing it from the non-state. Their approach was both historical and rational. To put it another way, they first attempted to determine how the state differs from the non-state analytically, and then they attempted to visualize the process by which the pre-statal situation gave rise to the statal, or, more specifically, how the state emerged from the non-state. The main solution to these two issues was discovered in the fish logic, or matasya nyaya doctrine.

In Hindu legal phraseology, Matsya-Nyaya, for example, is one expressive technical term. The ancient Indian philosophy known as Matsya-Nyaya makes reference to the Law of Fish. Literally interpreted, "Law of Fish" is "Matsya-Nyaya." The fundamental law of nature states that huge fish prey on small fish, or that the strong eat the weak. It bears similarities to the "Law of Jungle." Stated differently, the powerful will overcome the weak. To put it simply, the strong hold sway over the weak in times of chaos.

As we shall see, the foundation of Hindu idea of government was the conviction that human nature is depraved. Without a strong leader to keep men in check, the stronger may destroy the weaker. According to Kautilya, "If danda is not employed, it give rise to the condition of Matsya-

Nyaya, for the strong devour the weak in the absence of a chastiser." The Shanti Parva of the Mahabharata states, "Just as big fish devour smaller ones in water, so do strong people destroy weaker ones when the king carrying the rod of punishment does not protect the earth.".[34]

1.4.3 The State of Nature

Hooker argues that conflict is inherent in the state of nature. According to Hobbes, "the state of nature is indeed a state of war" and "the war of all against all". According to Spinora, the natural world exists in a condition of conflict and the right of might. Thus, the non-state is seen as anarchy and a conflict "between all against all." Each man in the non-state has one concept of right, two men have two concepts of right, and ten men have ten concepts of right. As thus, every man affirms his own definition of right and rejects that of every other man. They thus disparage one another."[35]

1.4.4 The Hindu Theory of State

The chief deity, Brahmadeva, considered the situation and concluded that human civilization can only endure if a legal system was established and upheld with the help of a monarch. Theories state that by giving humans a ruler, God assisted humanity in escaping the rules of the jungle. The ability to compel, restrict, and coerce makes a state what it is.

1. No danda, no state
2. No state, no dharma
3. No state, no property

1.4.5 Origin of State

There isn't any current evidence, nor is there likely to be any in the future, to shed light on this matter. To comprehend the conditions under which mankind initially affiliated themselves with a political organization, we have only the dim light of stories and myths. Ancient Indian institutions were often believed to have been established by divine activity, and the state was no different.

Though there are differences between the Digha Nikaya and the Mahabharta, there are sporadic theories on the state's beginnings. The Santiparvan continues, explaining that after a period of prosperity without a monarchy or laws, there occurred a moral decline.

Like the majority of ancient Indian philosophers, Hobbes believed that there was initially anarchy and that the state was an essential institution for the orderly life and advancement of society in the imperfect world as it is known to us from historical times. Docks asserts that the pre-government

[34] Benoy Kumar Sarkar, "The Hindu Theory of the State", Political Science Quarterly, Vol. 36, No. 1. (March 1921), pp. 79–90.

[35] *Ibid.*

era's natural state was roughly comparable to the Hindu mythology's Golden Age.

1.4.6 Elements of the State

In a monarchy, the king was seen as the cornerstone and essential component of rajya, determining the fate of the state. The statement "the king is (the basis of) the kingdom" (rajya rajyam) by Kautilya emphasizes this. In addition to rajya, the terms amatya and purva denote bureaucratic government, rastra land and population, danda military policy, and mitra foreign relations.

Arthashastra refers to janapada (slightly variant of rashtra) and durga (a fortified city).

There were four things which the state wished to promote, namely:

1. **Dharma:** morally right behaviours, respects towards Brahmans and elders
2. **Artha:** economic prosperity
3. **Kama:** everyday pleasures of the people
4. **Moksh:** spiritual enlightment/salvation

1.5 STATECRAFTS IN ANCIENT INDIA

State: Meaning and Definition

It is a political entity with the ability to interact with other nations on an equal footing, sovereignty over a defined region and the people that live there, and an efficient government. As per the Socialist theory of Max Weber (found in Public Administration and Bureaucrats theory). It is a political group that has been successful in staking claim to exclusive use of physical force, or violence, inside a certain area.

It's like breaking up the world into smaller parts. It is the most important political organization for a confined area and its inhabitants symbolize the residents of a territory's political independence and autonomy. Statecraft means the skilful management of the state affairs and statesmanship. But it denotes:

- Theory of origin of state
- Theory of kingship/rule
- Virtue, enterprise which a king should have
- How a king/ruler should maintain his state
- Political obligation: why people should obey the king/ruler
- Sources to understand the statecraft in Indian Political thoughts.

A state is a governmental unit that possesses the authority to govern a certain area and the people living in it, as well as the ability to interact with other states on an equal footing.

Statecraft

- The skilful management of state matters.
- Hindu scholars' attempt to distinguish the state from the non-state in order to comprehend it.
- Their approach was both historical and rational.
- They made an effort to look into how a state differs from a non-state.
- The state evolved from a non-state.

1.6 HINDU THEORY OF STATE

The circumstances surrounding that time, which are comparable to Hobbesian Leviathan, have led to it being referred to as the worst in human history. People contacted Lord Brahma, the creator, to free themselves from a life of torment because of the complete lawlessness of the situation, according to the Manusmriti. To uphold law and order and punish the wicked, the creator bestowed upon them the role of monarch.

Manu argues that the king was ordained by the Lord at a period of terror brought on by societal upheaval. Manu thus contends that the state was created suddenly rather than as an institution that developed over time.

Unlike ancient times, when the ruler's own judgment permitted the state, modern times find the state sanctioned by the judgment of society. The Danda idea actually transformed the state into a crystallized force during the eras of Manu and Kautilya.

Since the monarch is essentially a deity in human form, his divine concept of political duty was created to instill in the populace the idea that they should obey the king even when he is still a tiny child. He said that a king's duty was to punish wrongdoers because the threat of punishment was necessary to maintain social order. In return, the subjects were required to pay taxes, which were utilized by the king to establish a treasury and finance social welfare initiatives.

1.7 THE DOCTRINE OF MATSYA-NYAYA

The Matsya-Nyaya theory provided the primary remedy to each of these issues. "Nyaya" signifies reasoning, or the "logic of fish," and "Matsya" denotes fish. A non-state is a lawless society where people prey on one another and there is no justice. It is the worst kind of evil. The ancient Indians held that the monarch had to be a strong commander whose leadership was respected by everybody and that the position of kingship sprang from military need. Only when the nation's leader possesses strength, vigor, intelligence, and energy does success in battle become effortless. The Rigveda contains a section that seems to speak about the people (visas) choosing a king.[36]

'Matsya-Nyaya' literally means 'Law of Fish'. It is the fundamental law of nature that small fish become prey to big fish or the strong devour the weak. Human society will deteriorate into one that will either destroy or take advantage of the weaker members of society in the absence of government or the rule of law. One of the pioneers in Hindu political science history is Kautilya. According to Arthashastra, when a state is in formation, fish logic rules. The strong eat the weak when there is no one to administer punishment. To keep them clean, there should be a prey animal that is stronger than the others.

1.8 THE DOCTRINE OF DANDA

Danda has the power to impose restrictions, abolish social control, and act as an entity, a state remains what it is.

- When danda is absent, the natural condition, or Matsya-Nyaya, is what exists.
- Political theory discussions always place the notion of danda at the top because property and dharma are non-existent in non-state entities.
- Manu understood the Danda to be a comparable concept of unrestricted authority. Within Hindu political philosophy, danda is a two-edged blade that slashes in both directions.

1.9 STATECRAFT IN ANCIENT INDIA (HINDU THEORY OF STATE ORIGIN)

According to Manu's view of the state's formation, the disorder in the community caused dread, which is why the Lord established the king. The immortal particles of Indra, Pawan, Yama, Sun, Agni, Varun, Moon, and Kuber were combined to become King. He introduced a divine philosophy of political duty, which was designed to teach the people to obey the monarch when he was still a baby and to honor and venerate him as a human deity. Since the king's establishment was based on the protection of his subjects, this obligation is regarded as his fundamental responsibility. He is also supposed to uphold law and order and all castes. Given that the prospect of punishment was necessary to preserve social order, he identified punishing wrongdoers as a crucial responsibility of the monarch. In exchange, the subjects were required to pay taxes, which the king used

[36] A.S.Altekar, State and Government in Ancient India, Motilal Banarsidass Publishers Pvt. Ltd., 2001, pp. 75–76.

to fund social welfare programs and establish a treasury for hard times. A ruler who disobeys his obligations will die and go to hell.

According to Manu, the goal of government was to assist individuals in achieving prosperity, pleasure, and moral virtue (Dharma, artha, and karma). Therefore, in cooperation with his ministers, the monarch was expected to make a persistent effort to accomplish these goals. He was supposed to shield his people from external and internal threats and to ensure their safety. In addition to individuals who plotted unrest or were engaged in theft and robbery, internal adversaries also included unscrupulous government employees who misused their positions of authority to persecute the populace.

The state should uphold the general law, ensure that all varna obey their obligations (dharma), and maintain internal harmony inside the state independent of outside influence, according to Manusmriti. In addition to this, legislation regulating the cost of significant items should be made by the state.

The state has the authority to intervene in order to settle disputes or crises between various groups. The state also has a responsibility to ensure that its citizens receive a quality education and to provide for the needs of both instructors and students. In order to carry out these responsibilities, the king is also authorized to impose taxes and to punish anyone who stray from the straight and narrow. The Arthashastra of Kautilya is a notable treatise that was contributed to the world during the Mauryan Era in ancient India. It provides in-depth understanding of political manipulation.

He links the Saptanga or seven organs theory to the structure of the state, even if it is not exclusively based on Kautilya's facts or concept. A state is made up of seven different parts, each of which has a distinct function and is necessary for the state to function as a whole. Since Kautilya's cunning and brutal methods and policies reflected a strategy for statecraft that included warfare, he was dubbed as the Indian Machiavelli. "Might was right" and complete chaos are thought to characterize the state of "nature." The social contract theory developed by contratualists is not explicitly stated in Kautilya's Arthashastra. Kautilya doesn't use the deal to ascend to the throne either.

1.10 DIFFERENT HISTORICAL SOURCES TO UNDERSTAND THE STATECRAFT IN INDIAN POLITICS

Manusmiriti

- Written in the Manusmriti, sometimes called the Manav Dharmashastra, is the story of the mythical first man Manu and his pupil, most likely between 200 and 400 BCE. This Sanskrit text, originally translated into English by Sir William Jones in 1794, was used by the British colonial authority to develop Indian personal law.

Shanti Parva

One of the epic Mahabharat's eighteen books (Parvas), it is said to have been penned by the wise Ved Vyas.

- Most likely written between the third and fourth centuries BC and AD (CE).

Arthashastra

Arthashastra have been composed in the fourth century BC by "Kautilya," also known as "Chanakya" and "Vishnu Gupta."

Agganna Sutta

The 27th sutta in Digha Nikaya's Sutta Pitaka, or "Basket of Discourse,". It contains Buddhist ideas about the beginning of life, families, society, and the state.

Two clear streams—Brahminic (Hindu) and Shramanic (Buddhist).

Statecraft in Hindu Political thought

- "Matsya-Nyaya" (the law of fishes) indicated the state of nature.
- Divine to semi-divine view of state formation.
- There is a blurry line separating the government, society, and state.
- Dharma as the state's and society's universal moral code or set of laws.
- The distinction between the temporal and spiritual realms is unclear.

Statecraft in Buddhist Political thought

- The birth of the state notion of the social contract.
- The state is an ethical institution that derives its authority from the Dharma and guides people to live moral lives in this world and achieve salvation (Nibbana) in other (transcendental) worlds.
- It attempts to keep the two realms, Dharma and Ana, apart, but gradually merges them into the concept of Cakkavatti Dhammiko Dhammaraja (Chakravatri Samrat).

1.11 THEORY OF ORIGIN OF STATE [HINDU POLITICAL THOUGHTS]

1.11.1 Manusmriti

- **State of Nature:** life before the establishment of a formally structured state
- Similar to Hobbesian warfare of all against all, there was a state of war since there was no harmony, peace, or goodwill.

- It was Matsya-Nyaya who won; Anarchy, Might is Right.
- In order to escape their tormenting lives, people turned to Lord Brahma, who established the king in order to put an end to chaos and uphold law and order by punishing the evil and shielding the good.
- All significant gods' divine attributes were imbued in the king at creation.
- The moon's coolness, the sun's brilliance, Yama's rage, the wealth of Kuber, and the power of Indra

1.11.2 Mahabharta

- **Semi-contractual origin of the state/kingship:** Based on the necessity for peace and order in the society.
- **State of Nature:** At first, there was no state, no king, no punishment, no discipline, and no one to adjudicate or punish. People led to harmonious and happy life by following dharma.
- In the course of time, society degenerated. Lust and wrath maligned human virtue. Men left dharma and lost sight of right and wrong. Society plunged into Anarchy.
- Then the sages and Gods approached Vishnu (the Lord of Creation—Prajapati) and requested him to choose one among mortals who deserves to have superiority over the rest. Reluctantly, Vishnu gave the grist king—Virajas—some of his powers. However, in the dynasty of Virajas a corrupt ruler name Vena was born. The God removed Vena and made his son Prithu, the king.
- Accordingly an agreement reached between the king Prithu and rishis (sages) in the presence of Brahma—king to maintain peace, order, discipline, and foremost the Dharma.
- The ruler was given the oath for governance—fearlessly accomplish peace and order and all those tasks in which Dharma evenly resides. Disregarding what is dear and what not so, look upon all citizen with an equal eye.
- Rajya, Rastra, Janpad, Pura—terms used for denoting the state.

Thus, state originated by divine intervention, to maintain Peace, Order, Prosperity and Dharma. State enables achievement of individual and common Goods by ensuring each one performing his/her duties appropriate to his/her status and stage of life following Dharma.

1.11.3 Kautilya's Arthashastra, a Manual for Administrators

- With the establishment of the Mauryan rule, a systematic administrative set up came into vague in India.

- Kautilya or Chanakya, the prime minister of Chandragupta Maurya wrote the Arthashastra incorporating the teachings of earlier works on polity and administration.
- The Arthashastra incorporating the teachings of earlier works on polity and administration.
- Only passing reference (told by one spy to crowed)—not dealt in details.
- State of Nature—Matasya-Nyaya—Might is Right.
- This is because inherent weakness in human nature—lust, greed, striving for power/domination, ego, and selfishness.
- People tired of Matsya-Nyaya approached Manu to lead them as king, establish peace; order and Dharma
- For this, they agreed to give 1/6th of their grain and 1/10th of their profit from trade/business.
- Thus, state originated to maintain peace, order and welfare of the people.
- It does not support contractual theory of state origin.

1.11.4 Hindu Ideal of Kingship

Hindu kingship was the pinnacle of selflessness for the person whose honor it was to rule the Hindu people. The king's schedule, as prescribed by Kautilya, gives him only four and a half hours of sleep, three hours for meals and relaxation, and the remaining hours for state management. The monarch received instruction in the four fields of knowledge—philosophy (Anviksaki), economics (Varta), and governance science (Dandanithi)—so that he might competently carry out this duty.

In addition, the monarch had to learn self-control and defeat vanity, greed, lust, and rage. He was to avoid hunting, gambling, drinking too much alcohol, and women. Hindu rulers regarded their realm as a sacred trust rather than as their own property. Rana Sangram Singh, the Mewar monarch who was Sisodia, was a prime example of this philosophy. He once declared that he would abdicate his throne, comparing himself to a broken idol that is not suited to be worshipped because he had lost an arm, an eye, and one of his legs had been severely damaged.

However, the nobles and other officers talked him out of abdicating the throne, claiming that his physical limitations were caused by wounds he had while fighting bravery and valor that had allowed Mewar to win the day. As so, they declared that he was the most qualified individual to further the magnificence of that glorious throne. Therefore, according to the Mahabharatha, rulership is the highest dharma (duty) in society at all times.

Vedic Period

Vedic texts witnessed the existence of republican elements in Vedic polity. Where the institutions were existed individually and jointly indicating non-monarchial or aristocratic form of governments. The Puru kingdom the earliest vedic 'state', was formed by a 'super tribe' which joined several tribes in a new unit.

Early Vedic Period or Rigvedic Period (1500 BC-1000BC)

Political structure

Social grouping: kula (family)—brama – visu-jana

Tribal assemblies were called sabhas and samities

Example: Bharatas, Matsyas, Yadus

Social structure

Trade was conducted through the barter system but later on coins called nishka were in use.

Later Vedic Period or Painted Grey Ware Phase (1000 BC–600 BC)

Political structure

- Sacrifices were Rajasuya, Vajakeya and Ashwamedha Sabhas and Samities diminished.

Social structure

- Varna system became more distinct
- Women were not permitted to attend public assembly
- Gotras were institutionalized.

1.11.5 Jainism and Buddhism

- Buddhism and Jainism originated in Magadha, Bihar, and are still quite popular today.
- In Buddhism, the noble eightfold path is the path to end suffering. It practices right view, right aspiration, right speech, right action, right livelihood, right effort, right mindfulness, right concentration.
- Truth, non-violence, non-stealing, non-attachment, and control over cravings are the five vows of Jainism. They also adhere to the three gems of right action, right knowledge, and right perception.
- Jains trace their history and ideas back through a line of twenty-four pioneers.
- Buddhists adhere to their practices by following Aravindan Neelkandan.
- The Buddha's teaching was undoubtedly more socially inclusive than the Brahmanical varna-Jati philosophy.

1.11.6 Mahajanpadas and Magadha

- The first territorial idea was gradually strengthened in the sixth century BC with the rise of large states with towns as their seats of power. According to the traditional literature sixteen large states (mahajanpadas), each comprising several agricultural settlements (janapadas) existed in India in the sixth century BC. They are Kurum, Matsya, Assaka, Vajji, Malla, Gandhara, Kamboja, Magadh, Vatsa, Kosala, Shurasena, Panchal, Kurum, Matsya, Chedi and Avanti.[37]
- Distinct capital city, monarchs had organized troops, and taxes were gathered and referred to as "bhagga".
- The central feature of the republic government was its seemingly corporate character. The representatives of the tribes and the heads of families may have sat in the public assembly (santhagara) of the capital. It all started when the jana, or tribes, of the later Vedic era made the decision to establish their own geographical settlements.[38]
- The assemblies were dominated by oligarchs. This proves that republican system was in essence oligarchical.
- **Magadh:** One of the Second Urbanization's "Great Kingdoms" ruled by the Mauryan dynasty, Brikadrathad, Pradyota, Haryanka, and Shaishunga.
- **Geography:** Territory corresponded to the modern-day Patna and Gaya districts of the Indian states of Bihar.
- **History:** Lively accounts of Patliputra and Magadh are available in Indica and in travel diaries of Earian and Xuanrang.

1.11.7 The Mauryans and their World

As the Mauryas arrived in the later half of the 4th century, a plethora of data sheds light on the historical context. Control by a single force was the main goal, as the Mauryas occupied a sizable portion of the subcontinent. Expanding agriculture and increasing labor mobility were two strategies used to try to rebuild the empire. The Arthashastra was modeled after this effective and well-organized autocrat and civil service.

Mauryan Empire

- Patliputra (Imperial capital)
- Tosali (east)
- Ujjain (west)
- Suvarnagiri (south)
- Taxila (north)

[37] D.N. Jha, *Ancient India: In Historical Outline*, Manohar Publishers and Distributors, 2005. pp. 78.

[38] D.N. Jha, *Ancient India: In Historical Outline*, Manohar Publishers and Distributors, 2005. pp. 78.

Rulers

Chandragupta Maurya – Bindusara – Ashoka – Dasaratha Maurya – Samprati – Shalishuka – Devavarman – Shatadhanvan – Brihadratha

Social Structure

There were seven castes or groupings in Mauryan society. Among them were ranchers, farmers, philosophers, warriors, craftspeople, judges, and councilors.

Republics

Aristocracies and republics are non-monarchical forms of government. Tribes called the Halavas and Yaudheyas had republican governments as well. The term "gana" refers to a type of government where power is not held in a single individual but rather in a group of people, since gana had strong and distinct constitutionalism. Ancient India had a variety of non-monarchical states, as attested to by the insightful testimonies of several modern Greek writers.

Privileged Class in Republics: In ancient India, Brahmans have great social privileges. It would be demonstrated by Arthashastra IX that in certain republics, the military and the merchant classes held equal political power.

The governing class in the Gana stata was thus a fairly large one.

History

In the sixth century BC, there were republics in Madras, Purus, Panchals, Sibis, and Videhas. Historically speaking, republics were thriving in the northwest and northeast of ancient India. The Arjunayas thrived as a republican in the Agra-Jaipur region from 200 BC to 400 AD. The Punjab and the Indus valley were primarily the territory of republics from 500 BC to 400 AD.

1.11.8 Agriculture and Urbanization

Throughout the entire nation, agriculture has been the most common occupation. For the entirety of recorded history, agricultural practices have remained mostly unchanged worldwide. Consequently, a prevalent trait has been the conservatism that pursuing agriculture tends to produce. The framework of social and political life has not changed significantly because there hasn't been any significant economic shift. The form and character of the institutions have been somewhat determined by the supremacy of agriculture, which has also endowed them with impressive stability.

It is believed that urbanization started in India circa 600 BC and resulted in the establishment of the first historic cities. The monarchs of ancient and medieval India constructed a number of capital districts that eventually became towns.

It can be divided into:

1. Initial stage
2. Acceleration stage
3. Deceleration stage
4. Terminal stage

In the ninth and tenth mandalam of the Rigveda, the concept of politics, as it is understood in Indian historiography, is portrayed in a vague way. It then evolved and acquired basic contours in the Ramayana and Mahabharata, which reflected in the discussion of the state's organs of ideal forms. However, there is referred to as mythology and has historically not received scholarly recognition. Thus, political theory is derived from Digh Nikaya, and from its study, post-Buddha years saw the emergence of ideas about government, administration, and skill. In truth, Ambedkar maintained that the Buddha was the author of the majority of the mythical writings.

1.12 THEORIES OF ORIGIN OF KINGSHIP/STATECRAFT

1.12.1 State of Nature

- People abandoned their happy lives in which there was no private property and no family life, and pre-state social life became wretched.
- Among family members and personal belongings, vices were miserable things in life; they included vanity (empty pride), conceit, lust, greed, thievery, desire, crime, and punishment.
- Fed up with chaos, individuals select the most competent (i.e., most attractive, strong, and capable) member of the group to uphold order by punishing the evil and shielding the righteousness. People agreed to offer the great "elect," Mahasammata, one-sixth of their "rice" in exchange for this service.

The state or monarchy originated as a punitive establishment possessing exclusive authority to put an end to chaos and uphold law and order.

- Complementary to contractual Not Divine: The state is a necessary human organization; it is not divine.
- Only between the people and the government/king, for a specific purpose, and with reciprocal obligations; the king is to command and defend, uphold law and order, and the people are to obey and pay taxes.

1.12.2 Duties and Obligations of the King/Ruler According to Hindu Political Thought

- Preserving Dharma, peace, and order is the primary obligation.
- Safeguarding individuals against both external and internal threats.
- Maintain Dharma through appropriate Dandaniti.
- By upholding the Dharma by punishing the wicked, rewarding the good, and shielding the defenseless and innocent.
- A king is someone who protects and appeases his subjects. King is responsible for well-being and wealth of the state's population, and prioritizing the well-being and pursuits of his community before his own.
- The welfare and happiness of the king are entwined with that of the people.
- Apply Dandaniti's teachings of impartiality, rigor, and justice with fairness.
- View every citizen equally, disregarding what is valuable and what is not.
- Uphold and grow the state.

1.12.3 How a King should Behave: Kingly Virtues

The king should be believed to possess a portion of God, representing "Prajapati," the supreme deity on Earth, in a visible form. The king should be honest, reliable, and decent. It is important for him to be straightforward and honest, kind and understanding, but also realistic and objective. A king must control his senses and exercise self-control before he can subdue enemies and uphold the dharma in the lives of people. He should also be resourceful, enterprising, hardworking, vivacious, and enthusiastic.

- He should maintain righteous advisors, such as Raj Purohit, Ministers, and Councils.
- He should carry out yajna, or sacrifices for the upkeep, growth, and welfare of the people.
- Always ought to be a model for his people.
- The king should constantly strive to excel in his own domain and, by all means, vanquish his rivals and foes.
- His temperance ought to resemble the sun, clouds, or rain. He ought to adhere to the Dandaniti in order to uphold Dharma.

The life of a king is a mission, and he must constantly remind himself that he is a monarch simply to carry out his social duties and not to enjoy worldly luxuries. King is going to have to let go of his preferences. The monarch should always act impartially, bravely, and in accordance with Dharma. He should also always put the interests of his subjects before his own. In actuality, the monarch needs to treat his citizens impartially, as members of his own family, and he ought to discipline everyone, even his favorite person and sons.

1.12.4 Ceremonies Associated with Kingship

Ashvamedha parva of Mahabharata mentions that consecration (Rajyaabhisheka) was often followed by a digvijya (conquest), wherein the king sent his army to make sure of his sovereignty over the surrounding areas. Rajasuya ceremony consisted of the performance of a series of rituals like agnistoma, Panchavattiya, Indraturiya, Apamarga homa, Abhishekaaniya and others.

Constitutional Monarchy

The doctrine of divinity of the king was not known in the Vedic period. The people had a considerable share in the election of their king. Monarchy was almost elective in the Vedic period with the heads of kulas (tribes) having a voice in the election of the king.

A king should be a seeker of good (Sreya) rather than pleasure (Preya). He should be honest, reliable, and virtuous. He should be straightforward and conscientious, kind and hospitable, but impartial and pragmatic. A king should gather wisdom from a variety of sources and apply it so that moral laws are upheld. A monarch ought to uphold truth and ahimsa above everything else. A monarch who upholds the ideals of Rajadharma does not harbor animosity towards the weak, slight their adversaries, hate anyone, act hastily, or put off tasks.

1.13 DIFFERENT THEORIES OF ORIGIN OF STATE

1.13.1 Social Contract Theory

- The social contract theory, one of the popular explanations for the formation of states, holds that a contract between the king and his subjects is what gives rise to a state.
- Thus, it was expected of the newly anointed king to protect the nation and its citizens from outside threats and to provide law and order inside the realm. The earliest Vedic texts, however, made it clear that the monarch was chosen to lead an effective fight against the demons rather than asserting that the state was the outcome of the bargain.

1.13.2 Divine Origin Theory

- The theory of the state's and kingship's origins was not universally accepted in ancient Indian politics. This view held that society, not the king, produced the laws, and the king was subject to them. The people had valued the community more than the ruler. It was required of the king to act with affection and kindness, and he was not permitted to act indifferently.

- The epic Ramayana, one of India's greatest works of literature, also made it abundantly evident that the ruler was of divine descent and described the non-state area where people lived together like fish. However, some ancient scriptures, such as the Manusmriti, explain that the origin of state is from the divine one. An example from the Manusmriti is that "The lord created the king for the protection of his whole creation." The Mahabharata, another great epic, explains that a king is a person endowed with superior talent and caliber descended from heaven to king on earth.
- According to the Agni Purana, kings were incarnations or forms of Lord Vishnu, the earthly sustainer. Certain monarchs held titles such as Chakravarthi, which means "universal emperor," although certain Mauryan emperors bestowed titles like Devnampriya, which means "devotional emperor," onto them.

Divine elements of king created by God

- The theory of monarchal absolutism's "divine right" has long been invoked to support it. It asserts that a monarch has absolute or almost unlimited authority over his subjects because he is chosen by God and answerable to him alone. A ruler who disobeys his obligations will die and go to hell.
- People went to Lord Brahma, who established the king to put an end to anarchy and preserve peace and order, in order to be freed from their horrible lives. The king had celestial attributes when he was created. But the king was the best and only incarnation of God, who was compelled by conflict to uphold Dharma. He was also expected to uphold Dharma in interpersonal interactions. As a result, the state and the king were seen as divine creations.

1.13.3 Organic Theory

According to this view, every organ in the body serves a specific purpose and that states are similar to living things. The monarch, or sovereign, the minister, the land and people, the treasury, the army, the friends, and the allies are the seven components of the state. It is the monarch who is most significant among the seven components or sections.

Key Elements of State

Kautilya enumerated seven prakritis or essential organs of the state. They were as follows:

1. Swami (The Kuber)
2. Amatya (The Minister)
3. Janapada (The Population)
4. Durga (The Fortified Capital)
5. Kosha (The Treasury)
6. Danda (The Army)
7. Mitra (Ally and Friend)

According to this view, each organ in the body has a certain job to do and that states are similar to organisms. The theory maintains that each bodily part's optimal health and effective operation are essential to the organism's overall health. ***Shiva Neetisaara*** draws a comparison between the state and the human body. The king is the head, the minister is the eyes, according to Sukracharya. Footage is the territory, hands are the fout, army is the heart, and mouth is the gold. According to Mahabharta, every component is necessary for the state to function properly, and she concurs with this view.

1.14 DIFFERENT ASPECT OF INTERPRETATION OF INDIA

1.14.1 Political Interpretation of India

In ancient India, the ratio of the rural to the urban element was probably considerably higher than it is now. The population itself was considerably more dispersed than it is now because it was much smaller. Three million and a half people live in Kalinga, or roughly modern Orissa, according to the Hathigumpha inscription of Kharavela of Kalinga (c. 165 B.C.). Based on a comparative analysis between this figure and the data available for the Kalinga army and the number of casualties in a previous war, as well as a comparison with the number of armies provided for other regions and the current population of Orissa, the country's population is estimated to be approximately 100 million.

A situation like this can never be handled with certainty. However, the general signs point to a population of roughly one-third of what it is today in ancient India. As a result, it was far more widespread among older people than it is now. An environment like this did not foster the development of the intensity of life that defined some regions of ancient Greece and gave rise to democratic organization.

This fundamental prerequisite for democracy was not only absent, but representative democracy as a system of central administration was also unfeasible in its typical scale. Furthermore, caste disrupted the fundamental moral foundation of democracy by dividing the populace into at least four, and often many more, social, occupational, or social groups that are held in differing degrees of regard. Caste also attacked aristocracy as a system of government.

The intellectual, marital, and economic power of the community was distributed among different parts, and it demonstrated the concentration of power in one group, perhaps giving it the ability to rule the others. Monarchies remained the most prevalent form of government after democracy and aristocracy were abolished. When social, economic, and geographic variables come together, nothing else could match the circumstances. Any significant area of land could be united only through the monarchy.

Caste, which served as the cornerstone of the social order, was a major component in Hindu politics along with geography, race, and economic postulates. In addition to ruling out aristocracy or democracy as a system of government for the entire state, it had a significant impact on the characteristics, nature, and operations of the monarchial state. Caste resolves function into a meaning, a moral precept, or a religious idea. It essentially sacrifices individual values in the service of the group's exaltation. It almost feels like a denial of personality since it goes right to the core of uniqueness. It rejects the idea that each person is universal by nature and has the freedom to express himself wherever they see fit.

1.14.2 Geographical Interpretation of India

- The trend of Indian political history was driven by geographical factors.
- Although the Himalayas have created an impenetrable wall around the North, openings on the North-West have allowed in waves of immigrants and invaders who carried new institutions, ideas, and forms of civilization.
- Trade and general communication between India and the Middle East were made easier by the North Western Passes.
- Sir Aurel Stein's excavations and discoveries have demonstrated that the vast desert that supports inter-communication today was not as dry two millennia ago, and that prosperous centers of civilization once stood in Baluchistan and Sistan. These sites were abandoned, as the land gradually dried up, only after the second century BC.
- Within the frontiers of India there are hills and valley in the North, North-west, North-east, in central India and on the western coast, which offered shelter to hard-pressed tribes and clans.
- In the North, the vast Indo-Gangetic plains, flat and monotonous, have largely determined the form of political organisation.

During Vedic period Punjab was called "Sapta Sindhu" or "the land of seven rivers". During Vedic period Punjab included the area which was drained by the seven rivers were found. These rivers are—the Satluj, the Jhelum, the Ravi, the Beas, the Chenab, the Saraswati, and the Indus.

The seven rivers, opposed to the Saptarishi of the Avesta, are a group of seven major rivers of unknown or fluctuating identity. How the seven rivers were planned to be enumerated is not entirely clear. In northern India/eastern Pakistan, they are also found. If the Saraswati and five major Indian rivers are included (Sutlej, Ravi, Chenab, Jhelum, Beas, the latter all Indus tributaries), one river, possibly the Kubha, is absent. Other possibilities include the Arjikiya or Sushoma; see also the list of ten rivers in the Nadistuti sukta, both east and west of the Indus. Saraswati is referred to as "she with seven sisters" implying a group of eight rivers, with the number seven being greater than the individual members.

(i) The sapta-sindhu area was bounded in the east by Saraswati, in the west by the Sindhu, and Satudru, Vipasa, Asikni, Parusni and Vitasta were the five in between.
(ii) Sapta-Sindhu was referred to as the Persian Hapta-Hindu, etc.
(iii) The inhabitants of this area and civilization, the Sapta-Saindhavas, were called hapta-Haindavas by Persians, etc. The word is used in Zoroastrian Avesta.

- India in split into two halves by the Vindhyas and Satpuras. These chains of hills and mountains all free intercourse between the North on the one hand and the Deccan, and the country south of the Krisna on the other hand. But, they have served to make the two regions different in race, language and partly in culture.
- Agriculture has been the predominant occupation of the whole country. The method of agriculture has been practically the same everywhere and for the whole of recorded history.
- The conservation which the persuit of agriculture tends to produce has therefore been a common feature.
- The vast majority of the population have lived in scattered villages. The proportion of the rural to the urban elements was higher in ancient India.
- The mention of pasture and forest in Hindu literature leave the impression that the country was not so thickly populated. It distributed the intellectual, martial and economic strength of the community among various sections.
- Industry and commerce would be pursued by number of person in every locality. Industry has always shown a tendency to organise itself in guilds. In medieval Europe, Industry was carried on under a system of enterprise at once public and private, associative and individual.
- The unit of production was the workshop of the individual master craftsman; but the craftsman held his position as a master only by vritue of full membership in his craft guild.

1.14.3 Cultural Interpretation of India

- It must be admitted that a mass of men in a given religion often differ in important phychological traits from one another group. The innate characteristics have not been the same everywhere in India.
- The Tamil character has profoundly impressed the whole of South India. The temperament of the Marathas, who come closest to the Jeutons in their intellectual and moral makeup, differs significantly from that of the people of Bengal or Punjab.
- Yet, behind all the diversities, it is possible to discern some common characteristics. The Indian temperament displays an emotional flow and vibration which militates against rigidity of discipline and organisation and basis uniformity in associated life.
- The Buddhist Sangha which represented the maximum of organization in Hindu religious life, was persuaded by a spirit of intense localism. The Jaina orders were looser, while the Brahmanas seem to have been positively averse to ecclesiastical systematization.
- The lack of organization goes a long way to discount the Brahmanic chains to supremacy which fill Brahmanic literature.

1.14.4 Literary Interpretation of India

Historical compositions on law or polity are certainly numerous, but most are theoretical and do not readily provide information on the practical workings of institutions. General literature, whether religious or secular, provides insights only after the most thorough examination. The foreign accounts of India by classical, Chinese, and Arab writers are more valuable, but they are rare and some are not available to us in their original form. The inscriptions and coins discovered and deciphered by numerous scholars in increasing numbers lately constitute the real basis for studying the structure and functioning of Hindu political institutions. However, interpreting the administrative and fiscal terms in these sources presents significant difficulties. A discussion, based on scanty and dispersed materials, partly of uncertain dates, is bound to be perfunctory at best. Moreover, there is a risk of projecting modern or preconceived notions onto the terms and documents of ancient times, whose context is challenging to fully recapture. One might be tempted to dismiss the polity of ancient India as mere "Oriental Despotism," requiring no further analysis or evaluation. Alternatively, one might inaccurately ascribe the spirit and ideals of modern times to antiquity. Again, such is the nature of our documents that isolated statements readily adapt themselves to attractive hypotheses and generalisations. The warning uttered by Professor Keith in regard to the Rigveda applies to much else in the rage of Hindu literature, epigraphy and numismatic. It is easy, he writes, to frame and support by plausible evidence and various hypotheses, to which the only effective objection is that other hypotheses are equally legitimate and that the facts are too imperfect to allow or conclusions being drawn. Caution, indeed, must be the governing principle of all endeavours to elucidate the political institutions of the ancient Hindus. Another caution, equally essential is to resist the ever-present temptation of "combining information". A picture, constructed from texts separated by hundreds or thousands of years may be fascinating in its fullness but may not be true of any given each. Similarly, documents from regions far apart cannot be used for a single area. In the uncertainty of dates and the obscurity of the whole subject, every document should, as a general rule, be handled by itself and then joined to others only on the surest possible ground. The application of the most rigid critical standards alone can serve to illuminate the subject and, it may be, to add a new chapter to the science of comparative politics.

Geographical Interpretation of Ancient India by Beni Prasad

Different sources of ancient India are historical compositions, work on law or polity, general literature, religious or secular. Foreign narratives about India found on coins, inscriptions, and works by classical, Chinese, and Arab authors. Professor Keith cautions against grafting the spirit and ideals of current times into antiquity or writing away the political system of ancient India as merely "Oriental Despotism" without more investigation. The nature and working of Hindu political institutions were largely affected by geography, racial characteristics, social organizations and economic conditions. The most important is the geographical factors. Himalaya formed an impenetrable wall on the North, where as North-West proved to be a gateway for successive borders of immigrants and invaders who brought new type of civilization, new ideas and institutions which facilitated commercial and general intercourse in India[39].

Recent excavations by Sir Aurel Stein proved that the extensive desert which bars inter-communication at present was not so arid 2000 years ago.

In Baluchistan and Sistan there existed flourishing sites of civilization which were abandoned with gradual drying of land after 2 century B.C.

Northern region is the vast plain with indo-gangetic plains, flat and monotonous determined the form of political organization.

Zimmern in Greece said "each little plain, rigidly sealed within its mountains barriers, and with its population concentrated upon its small portion of good soil, seems formed to be a complete world of its own. Make your way up the pasture land, over the pass and down on to the fields and orchards on the other side, and you will find new traditions and customs, new laws and new Gods and most probably a new dialect. You will be in a new nation".[40]

---

[39] *Ibid.*
[40] *Ibid.*

North India is safe since there are no mountains, lakes, or pricey rivers to threaten the stability of governmental borders. Political theory and public opinion resemble a great kingdom extending to the sea—a universal dominion that every state aspires to. Consequently, states often seek to encroach upon their neighbors. The formation and operation of governmental institutions are influenced by constant battle or preparedness for warfare, which supports monarchy over other forms of governance.

Regional self-governance would generally prevail. The Vindhyas and Satpuras divide the Deccan region of India in half. These mountain ranges permit unrestricted travel between the nation south of the Krishna and the north and deccan, popularly known as table land, make the two areas distinct in terms of language, race, and some degree of culture. The Deccan Plateau is geographically distinct from the extreme south, and it is substantially different in terms of race, language, and culture.

Political division: India is divided into three major regions: the north, the south, and the Deccan area as a whole. Its civilization has persisted on its own for thousands of years despite contact and influence from the Aryans. There is not much Aryan blood mingled in. The language uses very few vocabulary from Sanskrit. The political institutions differ in a number of significant ways.[41]

The Indian subcontinent's southwest is known as the Malabar Coast. Generally speaking, it refers to India's western coast, stretching from Konkan to Kanyakumari. Geographically speaking, it encompasses the entirety of Kerala and the Kanara region of Karnataka, two of the wettest areas on the subcontinent in the far southwest of India, protected from external influences by the sea and the western mountain. A small area of land known as the konkan is surrounded by the sea and the Western Ghats, which allowed it to maintain and grow its unique institutions. Though it is a separate country, the island of Sinhala, sometimes known as Ceylon, is politically and historically connected to southern India and, to a lesser extent, to India overall.

The north, the Deccan, the south, and Ceylon should be addressed separately in any administrative survey. Nevertheless, they have often impacted one another. Additionally, some conditions were comparable, which made their circumstances similar in some ways. The area of economic life is where the north of India and the rest of the nation most closely resemble each other. The majority of the workforce in the entire nation was employed in agriculture. Agriculture has been practiced almost everywhere using essentially the same techniques. Their own shape and personality were somewhat shaped by the dominance of agriculture.

The great bulk of people have lived in dispersed settlements. In ancient India, the ratio of rural to urban areas was significantly larger than it is

---

[41] *Ibid.*

today. The Hathigumpha inscription (transl. "Elephant Cave" inscription) of Kharavela is situated near Udayagiri, around 5 kilometers (3.1 mi) west of Bhubaneswar international airport. Among the subjects covered in the Hathigumpha Inscription is the biography of a monarch who ruled over an area of ancient India that is today in or close to Odisha in the east. It also contains details on public works initiatives, religious principles, the goals of military expeditions, society, and culture.

Form of Government

The typical size of a state and communication barriers make direct or representative administration as a type of central authority implausible. Caste divided people into at least four and usually more racial, occupational, and social groupings, undermining the fundamental morality of democracy. The aristocracy was also harmed by caste since it prevented the accumulation of power in one group that may allow it to rule over the others. All by itself, it might represent the unification of a huge geographic area. Group members who become mindful of how their affiliation with a group affects their place in society is known as group consciousness. The village, which shares in the common culture of the region, is the social and political unit of supremacy in agriculture. It would usually seem like a world unto itself in the course of everyday living. Its collective consciousness would grow stronger in all aspects. By combining an increasing number of villages together, a higher division of local government may be formed.

1.14.5 Racial Interpretation of India

Although racial influences are difficult to pinpoint, it is still true that most males in a given area frequently differ from other groups in significant psychological ways. Tamil character, for example, is distinct and has influenced south India profoundly. The Marathas are not at all like the people who live in Bengal or Punjab. Even said, there are a few traits that set Indians apart from people in other nations quite strongly when taken as a whole.

It was rare for a caste or a sub-caste to have a distinct legislative, executive, or judicial apparatus. The Brahmanic literature is repleted with claims to dominance, which are largely discounted by the disarray. Hindus' political lives are greatly influenced by caste. Social laws' foundation was discovered. It had a profound effect on the structure, dynamics, and nature of the monarchical state. Function is resolved into a goal, an ethical precept, or a religious idea. Values of the individual are sacrificed by caste.

The caste system's tenet is the denial of human dignity. It has an impact on the government's makeup as well. It would hand over power to the Kshatriyas. The king was frequently accompanied by Brahman priests and ministers. Brahmana parsihads or committees were frequently tasked with resolving legal issues. Every group that has attained consciousness tends to be autonomous or almost autonomous within its own domain. It promotes the inclination toward functional organization. The goal of religion was to influence the rulers' lives as well as those of the general populace. It taught the king to be kind, compassionate, and to strive for the welfare of the people. It was spiritually superior to the state. Politics was likely to be affected by changes in religion. Many emperors abdicated in favor of their sons or relatives as a result of religious teachings emphasizing renunciation of the world. Coins, a few seals, the ruins of ancient towns and buildings, caves, and the narratives of foreign observers (Arab, Greek, and Chinese) and Hindu chronicles or biographies like the Vikramankadevacharita of Bilhana, the Rajatarangini of Kalhana, and the Harshcharita of Banabatta are added to the epigraphic records. Indian sources were enhanced by Hindu literature, Sanskrit, blended Sanskrit, Pali, Brahmanic, Buddhist, and Jaina texts.[42]

MODEL QUESTIONS FOR PRACTICE

1.1 What do you mean by state? What is the difference between state and Nation?

1.2 Analyze the theory and Practice of 'Ancient Indian Statecraft'.

1.3 Define the Hindu theory of State by Benoy Kumar Sarkar.

1.4 What is Matsyay-Nyaya? What is its relevance in Ancient India?

1.5 Define the meaning of state in Ancient India by Beni Prasad.

1.6 Describe the theories of origin of Kingship and Statecraft.

1.7 Describe the Kautilya concept of State in 'Ancient times'.

1.8 What are the state origin theories in context to Ancient India?

1.9 How would you define the India's political, social, geographical, literary and racial interpretation of Ancient India?

1.10 What are the different historical sources to study statecraft in ancient Indian politics?

---

[42] *Ibid.*

2

Concept of Dharma

2.1 INTRODUCTION

"When the nations of the earth were sent forth one after the other, a special work was given by God to each, the word which each was to say to the world, the peculiar word from the Eternal which each one was to speak. As we glance over the history of nations, we can hear resounding from the collective mouth of the people this word, spoken out in action, the contribution of that nation to the ideal and perfect humanity. To Egypt in old days, the word was Religion; to Persia the word was Purity; to Chaldea the word was Science; to Greece the word was Beauty; to Rome the word was Law; and to India, the eldest-born of His children, to India He gave a word that summed up the whole in one, the word *Dharma*. That is the word of India to the world."[1]

—*Annie Besant, Convention of the Theosophical Society, 1898*

The significance of *Dharma* is remarkably captured by Annie Besant in her address during the annual convention of the Theosophical Society in 1898 by highlighting several integral points:

(i) The term *Dharma* and the notions underlying the term centrally defines the Indic civilization as internalized in the thought and culture of India.

(ii) *Dharma* is an essence which is unique to India and is also the concept which represents India in the world. It is "that which India was meant to teach"[2] the world. It is interesting to note that *Dharma* does not have any cognate term in Indo-European language family including Avestan and was possibly "a

---

[1] Annie Besant, *Dharma,* Theosophical Publishing House, Madras, 1964, p. 1.

[2] *Ibid.,* p. 9.

neologism invented by the poets of the regvedic hymns."[3] Mrs. Besant's address went on to further explain *Dharma,* frequently emphasizing the mystery, complexity and difficulty in confining the term to a fixed definition. *Dharma,* according to her is "the inner nature, which has reached in each man at a certain stage of development and unfolding. It is this inner nature which moulds the outer life, which is expressed by thoughts, words, and actions, the inner nature which is born into the environment suited for its further growth."[4] Therefore, *Dharma* is subjective in nature, for the environment for each human being is different and one, who performs actions (*karma*) according to one's own innate nature, aligns with *Dharma*. *Dharma* is thereby inextricably woven with actions and hence the word is often translated as duty, morality, law, righteousness or religion. While it means all of these and many more, the meaning is deeper and wider that these translations express.

2.2 DHARMA: AN OVERVIEW OF HISTORIOGRAPHY

Dharma is probably one of the most exhaustively discussed and debated subjects among scholars of Indian literary history. It is evident from the above discussion that *Dharma* became an essential component of discourse in India by the late 19th century. However, discussions on the subject may be traced back from the late 18th century with the English translation of the *Manusmṛti,* also known as the *Mānava Dharmaśāstra* by Sir William Jones in 1776.[5] The *Manusmṛti* was in fact one of the first Sanskrit texts to be translated into English and the primary motivation to translate the text was to gather knowledge about Hindu customs by the British in order to administer the population.

The writings on *Dharma* in this period prominently identified it as "Hindu Law". Studies on the *Dharma* began in India fairly as a part of the larger historical exercise during the colonial period in India. The initial thoughts and investigations on early Indian jurisprudence and specifically Hindu Law emerged apparently with the western scholarship and its notion of law and simultaneously and more significantly as a part of the major colonial requirement to administer the Hindus. However, specifically academic, systematic and objective writings on Indian legal History started when the scholars of jurisprudence and historians of law besides trying

---

3 Patrick Olivelle, "Dharmaśāstra: A Textual History" in Timothy Lubin, Donald R Davis Jr. and Jayanth K. Krishnan (ed.), *Hinduism and Law: An Introduction,* Cambridge University Press, UK, 2010, p. 31.

4 Annie Besant, Dharma, Theosophical Publishing House, Madras, 1964, pp. 8–9.

5 Gavin Flood, *An Introduction to Hinduism,* Cambridge University Press, Cambridge, 1996, p. 56.

to trace the historical roots of Indian legal consciousness and its antiquity also began debating if the concept of "*Dharma*" can be considered as a formal system of rules usually enforced through a set of institutions that gives it the force of law and thereby government of the society through those institutions.

Considering the fact that *Dharma* crucially defined the ancient Indian civilization, it has been a subject of serious research ever since the emergence of organized study of Indian history. The initial years of study on *Dharma* revolved around an attempt to define and translate the term. Studies soon revealed the degree of difficulty in translating the term with scholars' often labeling *Dharma* as 'untranslatable'. However, it was realized that since the meaning of the term *Dharma* gets highly altered based on context, genre of text or religious tradition, it cannot be rendered into any exact equivalent. In other words, the word *Dharma* is used in a variety of meanings, for example, just as *Dharma* may correctly translate into law or justice, it may equally be correct to translate it into morality, virtue, teaching, justice, sacrifice, nature, foundation, and religion and so on. Therefore, it has been a long time since the broad semantic range of *Dharma* has been recognized by scholars.

Further studies introduced fresh insights by shifting the focus to explain the validity *Dharma* as a legal concept. Scholars began debating on the extent to which *Dharma* could qualify as 'law' and how far the *Dharmaśāstras* could be considered as 'codified legal texts'. Scholars like Robert Lingat[6], Duncan Derrett[7], Werner Menski[8] and A.D. Mathur[9] are considered important contributors in this discussion.

Robert Lingat was one of the first to initiate a systematic discussion on the subject. Though he denied *Dharma* to be positive law because of absence of any formal legislation preceding the codification of the *Dharmaśāstras*, he believes that *Dharma* can still qualify as law since it bound individuals within their respective rules. Moreover, within the practical realm it is through *Dharma* that justice was also dispensed. Duncan M. Derrett, advanced the study of *Dharma* to demonstrate the role of the *Dharmaśāstra* texts in practice in resolving disputes in reality. Several of his articles give an interesting account of the actual application of the *Dharma* norms texts in resolving long standing disputes.

---

6 Robert Lingat, *The Classical Law of India*, Munshiram Manoharlal Publishers Pvt. Ltd., 1993.

7 J. Duncan Derrett, "Two Inscriptions Concerning the Status of Kammalas and the Application of Dharmaśāstra" in *Essays in Classical and Modern Hindu Law,* Vol. 1, Leiden E.J. Brill, 1976.

8 Werner Menski, *Hindu law: Beyond Tradition and Modernity*, Oxford University Press, New Delhi, 2003.

9 Ashutosh Dayal Mathur, *Medieval Hindu Law: Historical Evolution and Enlightened Rebellion,* Oxford University Press, 2007.

Contrary to the previous assumptions of *Dharma* qualifying as law, Menski argued that ancient India was not controlled by a uniform system of law. He argues that since in a large part of the India law prevailed as customs and hence unwritten, Hindu law should never be reconstructed totally by merely looking at the *sāstric* or written texts alone. He also eschews legal uniformity in traditional Hindu legal system considering the absence of a strong political center for most of Indian history. Mathur also does not accept *Dharma* as law; instead he considers *vyavahāra* to be what can be called as law. He argues that *Dharma* sets the outer limit of law as well as forms its core in the sense that *Dharma* subsumes and propounds the philosophical notions such as the concepts of justice, equity or good conscience. In this way *Dharma,* he says, can certainly be taken to form the basis of law and forward the very purpose of the formation of law but it cannot be understood as equivalent of law.

Another important contribution in the study of *Dharma* came with a series of reflections on the historical background in which the *Dharmaśāstra* literature was produced. Wendy Doniger[10] and Patrick Olivelle[11] in their translations of the *Manusmṛti* have studied the prevailing historical conditions in which the text was written. Doniger explains the composition of Manu within a deep socio-political crisis which came with the decline of the Vedic Brahmanic ideals because of the rise of the heterodox cults in India. Manu emerged as a major revaluation of the old Vedic customs which incorporated several significant changes to render flexibility to orthodox Brahmanism and ensure its survival. Olivelle argues on similar lines but particularly asserts the emphatic Buddhist presence in the society and a resultant decline of the *brāhmaṇas* for the composition of the text. Their studies are important because they explain the remarkable evolution in the nature and meaning of *Dharma* with the emergence of this genre of literature and hence add another dimension to our understanding of *Dharma.*

The edited volume titled *"Dharma: Studies in its Semantic, Cultural and Religious History"*, by Patrick Olivelle[12] serves as another significant contribution in the study of *Dharma* both in terms of methodology and fresh insights into the subject. The book allows one to believe that despite years of scholarly engagement with the subject, there remains a tremendous scope to understand the term and the concept.

From the brief overview above, what appears is that though the broad semantic range of the word *Dharma* was identified by scholars but no

---

[10] Wendy Doniger and Brian K. Smith (tr.), *The Laws of Manu*, Penguin Books, 1990.

[11] Patrick Olivelle (tr.), *Manu's Code of Law: A Critical Edition and Translation of the Mānava Dharmaśāstra,* Oxford University Press, New Delhi, 2004.

[12] Patrick Olivelle (ed.), *Dharma: Studies in its Semantic, Cultural and Religious History,* Motilal Banarsidass Publishers Private Limited, Delhi, 2009.

attempt was made to explain the various historical processes through which the word acquired those meanings and definitions. The present collection of essays crucially contributes in this direction by attempting to explain the evolution of the term and hence the expansion in the meaning of the word.

As an edited volume, it contains a multitude of contributors, covers a fairly long-time period and uses a wide range of textual material. The essays seek to identify the junctures at which *Dharma* goes through an innovation and alteration in meaning and definition. Each essay contributes towards adding an additional dimension to the meaning and usage of the term.

Further, the overview also indicates that studies on *Dharma* were focused on the Brahmanical sources in general and *Dharmaśāstra* literature in particular. The present collection is pioneering in the sense that texts from various traditions like Brahmanical, Buddhist and Jain are juxtaposed and examined instead of studying any particular text in isolation. This method comes from the assumption of the scholars that different socio-political, religious or philosophical traditions influence each other since they are in constant dialogue with each other. Both negation and acceptance of each other's worldview has an impact on the way terms acquire different understandings which in turn leads to the semantic development of the term. Olivelle in his essay observes that "it is important to recognize that words do not exist in a vacuum; they are used by individuals and groups that have their own histories and interests and that change the meanings of words as they use them."[13] Thus, the book gives unique insights as to how traditions select terms from the prevailing vocabulary of the society and use them in conventional ways as well as redefine them in entirely newer ways.

Paul Horsch's essay entitled "From Creation Myth to World Law"[14] serves as a useful starting point since he starts from the earliest literary texts. He uses the Vedic literature, the *Brāhmanas* and the *Upaniṣads* to trace the origin of *Dharman (Dharma)* and the subsequent changes in its meaning up to the emergence of Buddhism. He begins by explaining the etymological meaning of *Dharman*, which is *dhṛ* and which means 'to hold', 'to support' or 'to maintain'. Unlike Grabmann, who had rendered about 20 meanings of *Dharman* in the *Ṛigveda*, Horsch suggests that in the *Ṛigveda*, the root meaning of *dhṛ* survived entirely in the older passages and is unnecessary to expand the semantic range of *Dharman* at this stage. He observes that at the earliest stage, *Dharman* was used in the context of a

[13] Patrick Olivelle (ed.), *Dharma: Studies in its Semantic, Cultural and Religious History*, Motilal Banarsidass Publishers Private Limited, Delhi, 2009, p. 85.

[14] Paul Horsch, "From Creation Myth to World Law" in Patrick Olivelle (ed.), *Dharma: Studies in its Semantic, Cultural and Religious History*, Motilal Banarsidass Publishers Private Limited, Delhi, 2009.

mythical cosmic act in which the cosmos came into being when the Vedic gods like Indra and Varuṇa separated the sky and the earth and provided 'support' to the sky so that it does not fall down. In the next stage the sense of *Dharman* transforms to indicate a continuous act of 'supporting' so that cosmic stability can be incessantly maintained. Subsequently, *Dharman* transforms into an independent and autonomous force which indicated the 'maintenance' of cosmic and social order.

A profound transformation in meaning occurs at the next stage when *Dharman* is detached from the mythical action and the notion enters the human social level where human beings are expected to participate in the maintenance of the cosmos by performing the cultic ceremonies such as the fire sacrifices. Horsch suggests that it is at this stage that *Dharman* becomes 'world law'. This meaning of *Dharman* becomes more profound in the Later Vedas and the term changes from *Dharman* to *Dharmaḥ* in the *Atharvaveda*. Since the *Brāhmana* era, *Dharma* changes into various duties and rights of individuals and castes. Horsch suggests that it is the Later Vedic meaning 'world law' that Buddhism uses to explain that conformity to laws of world events leads to liberation or salvation. Further the Buddhists also elevated this rendering of *Dharma* to a divine/theistic platform.

The essay by Joel P. Brereton titled '*Dharman* in the *Ṛigveda*'[15]. Unlike Horsch, Brereton only focuses on the *Ṛigveda* as his source and analyses the passages in which the term *Dharman* occurs, either independently or in compounds like *Satyadharman*, *Dharmavant*, *Dharmakṛt*. Out of the sixty three times that the term occurs in the *Ṛigveda*, Brereton observes an increasing frequency in the younger layers which suggests that *Dharman* was a developing terminology. Unlike Horsch, he concludes that there is very little change in the meaning of *Dharman*. He believes that it is unnecessary to inflate the semantic range of *Dharman* to support, uphold or maintain. Instead, he suggests that it is reasonable to use the term 'foundation' to account for its usage in most cases.

Patrick Olivelle's 'The Semantic History of *Dharma*: The Middle and Late Vedic Periods'[16], as the title suggests, deals with the texts of the mid and late Vedic periods. He studied the selected *Yajurvedic Saṃhitās*, the *Brāhmaṇas*, the *Āraṇyakas*, the *Upaniṣads*, the *Śrautasūtras* and the *Gṛhasūtras*. He suggests that considering the centrality that *Dharma* attains during the said period, one would expect an increase in the frequency and semantic range of the term in these literature. On the contrary, he observes that both

---

[15] Joel P. Brereton, "*Dharman* in the *Ṛegveda*", in Patrick Olivelle (ed.), *Dharma: Studies in its Semantic, Cultural and Religious History*, Motilal Banarsidass Publishers Private Limited, Delhi, 2009.

[16] Patrick Olivelle, "Semantic History of *Dharma*: Middle and Late Vedic Periods", in Patrick Olivelle (ed.), *Dharma: Studies in its Semantic, Cultural and Religious History*, Motilal Banarsidass Publishers Private Limited, Delhi, 2009.

its frequency as well as its semantic range decreases in the Later Vedic literature. He shows that *Dharma* acquired a specialized meaning during this period within the Brahmanical literature and it was this specialized rendering that was adopted by the Buddhists and the Mauryan king Aśoka. After their adoption, they expand the semantic range of *Dharma* by defining the term in a variety of ways. This expanded notion of *Dharma* is subsequently adopted and incorporated within the later Brahmanical literature. The specialized meaning that *Dharma* acquires within the Later Vedic corpus related majorly to the king, royal sacrifices and several other royal symbols. Olivelle points out that in the *Yajurvedic Saṃhitās* a clear connection is drawn between *Dharma* and Varuṇa within important ritual contexts such as *rājasuya* and *aśvamedha* sacrifices. Moreover, royal power or *kṣatra* as well as judicial spheres are also intimately connected to *Dharma*. Olivelle suggests that it is this specialized *Dharma* that Buddha borrows from traditional Brahmanical notions and articulates his religious ideology. Subsequent to this adoption, *Dharma* becomes a part of the religious vocabulary and becomes more ethicized and righteous. This semantic development of the term is further strengthened by Aśoka who associated *Dharma* with several other concepts such as morality, virtue, non-violent, etc. An inflated understanding of *Dharma* is finally adopted by Brahmanical religion leading to the emergence of the corpus of *Dharmasūtra* and *Dharmaśāstra* literature.

The essay by Rupert Gethin titled "He Who Sees *Dhamma* Sees *Dhammas*: *Dhamma* in Early Buddhism"[17] is essentially an understanding of the meanings of *Dharma* that developed internally within Early Buddhism. He examines the early Buddhist literature like the *Nikāyas* and early Abhidhamma texts. He identifies six different meanings of *Dhamma* which can be identified in these texts. They are: the 'teaching' of the Buddha, 'good conduct' in general but specifically the conduct prescribed by the Buddha, the truth realized by following the Buddhist path, particular nature or quality, the underlying natural law or order and the basic mental or physical state or thing. Gethin observes that the basic Brahmanical and Buddhist understanding of *Dharma* are similar since both describe nature of reality and also controls the actions of individuals. However, a development in the meaning of *Dhamma* is comprehended when it describes the process of Buddha's way of contemplation, meditation and experience. Therefore, the Buddhist notion of *Dhamma* based on basic mental and physical quality which is also called the Buddhist theory of *Dhammas* is the specific addition to the meaning of *Dharma* within the early Buddhist literature.

[17] Rupert Gethin titled "He Who Sees *Dhamma* Sees *Dhammas*: *Dhamma* in Early Buddhism" in Patrick Olivelle (ed.), *Dharma: Studies in its Semantic, Cultural and Religious History*, Motilal Banarsidass Publishers Private Limited, Delhi, 2009.

"*Dharma* in Jainism—A Preliminary Survey"[18] by Olle Qvarnstrom, studies the meanings of *Dharma* in the Jain tradition. The author says that the most frequent use of the term is in the sense of Jain teachings which as evidenced in the early canonical Sanskrit texts *Ācārangasūtra* and *Sūtrakṛtāngasūtra*. Gradually, within the tradition *Dharma* began assuming additional meanings. The *Tattvārthasūtra* of *Umāsvāti* and *Pravacanasāra* of Kundakunda written between 150–350 AD, designate ten constituents of righteous behavior as *Dharma*. These texts also emphasize on adopting a particular state of mind to be able to practice moral conduct. Olle suggests that such development in the meaning of *Dharma* within Jain tradition was taking place because of the maturity into Jainism as a religion. He also says that the contemporary Brahmanical religion and culture expressed in the *Dharmaśāstra* influenced the Jain understanding of *Dharma*.

Richard W. Lariviere's "*Dharmaśāstra*, Custom, 'Real Law' and 'Apocryphal' *Smṛtis*"[19] is a significant contribution not only in the present volume but also within the larger debate on the validity of *Dharma* as law and the *Dharmaśāstras* as law codes. Lariviere in this essay argues against Lingat's and Derrett's understandings of *Dharma* in the *Dharmaśāstras*. He contends that *Dharmaśāstras* should be understood as representing a record of local customs and traditional standards of behavior instead of conventional and western concept of law. To him, *Dharma* and *Dharmaśāstra* fit in more particularly as sources of law. He objects to Derrett's opinion that *Dharmaśāstra* is not positive law and instead argues that these texts qualify as positive legal treatise because their provisions are based on normative values and are enforced by a properly constituted authority. He cites the verse from *Nāradasmṛti* which tells us that the king id obliged to enforce even the customs of the heretics. This citation qualifies Lariviere's understanding of *Dharma* as localized or specific customs and the *Dharmaśāstras* as representing positive laws. He explains *Dharma* as a record of local customs in the background of Brahmanization of several geographic areas and tribes. Therefore, no matter how far the *smṛtis* did not approve of any customary practices had to incorporate within the text so as to facilitate uniformity and better administration.

John Brockington's "The Concept of *Dharma* in the *Rāmāyaṇa*"[20] studies the evolution of meanings of *Dharma* in the epic *Rāmāyaṇa*. Brockington, had previously argued that the Vālmīki *Rāmāyaṇa* developed into its received

---

[18] Olle Qvarnstrom, "*Dharma* in Jainism—A Preliminary Survey" in Patrick Olivelle (ed.), *Dharma: Studies in its Semantic, Cultural and Religious History*, Motilal Banarsidass Publishers Private Limited, Delhi, 2009

[19] Richard W. Lariviere, "Dharmaśāstra, Custom, 'Real Law' and 'Apocryphal' *Smṛtis*" in Patrick Olivelle (ed.), *Dharma: Studies in its Semantic, Cultural and Religious History*, Motilal Banarsidass Publishers Private Limited, Delhi, 2009

[20] John Brockington, "The Concept of *Dharma* in the *Rāmāyaṇa*" in Patrick Olivelle (ed.), *Dharma: Studies in its Semantic, Cultural and Religious History*, Motilal Banarsidass Publishers Private Limited, Delhi, 2009

form in five stages which can be discerned from the linguistic analysis of the text. In this essay, he tries to identify the semantic development in the meaning of *Dharma* on the basis on his five-stage theory. He observes that out of the 1100 occurrences of the term in the text, the second stage of development of the epic shows the highest frequency. In the first stage, the meaning of *Dharma* is closer to the Vedic understanding of the word while in the second stage the emphasis shifts to religious matters and *Dharma* is understood in terms of ethical behavior. In majority of the occurrences, it denotes morality, virtue, family, personal duties, *rājadharma*, duties of caste, etc.

"*Dharma* and its Translation in the *Mahābhārata*"[21] by James L. Fitzgerald summarizes the meanings in which *Dharma* can be understood in the *Śāntiparvan* of the *Mahābhārata*. Rather than translating the word differently in different contexts, he preferred to understand the underlying concept of *Dharma* and accordingly categorize the term into three meanings. The first meaning of the term, which he calls the 'the Basic Theme of *Dharma*' signifies normative action that is beneficial to the agent after death. This usage refers to the actions of the agents such as performance of sacrifices, generating offspring, hospitality to guests, honoring the *Veda*, pilgrimage etc. The second sense denotes the 'ethical quality' of some action, for example, rightness, goodness, the quality of correctness, justice etc. The third usage of the term falls in the category of *Sādhāraṇa Dharma* which means the inner qualities (*guṇas*) of a person which includes attributes such as virtue, generosity, kindness, honesty, etc.

2.3 BUDDHIST INTERPRETATION OF *DHAMMA*

The Bhuddhist's *Dhamma* intended for individuals to overcome *dukkha*, or human pain or unhappiness. The *Dhamma* reveals the truths as taught by the Buddha. By doing this, people are also offered a way of life that can aid them on their journey towards enlightenment. Buddhists are urged to practice meditation and the Noble Eightfold Path. Buddhists believe that they can be freed from suffering by regularly putting the *Dhamma* into practice. The *Dhamma*, the Sangha, and the Buddha are revered in Buddhism.

The *dhamma*, or teachings of the Buddha, addressed basic questions concerning the nature of existence, the human predicament, and the self. The Buddha also emphasized the need of upholding moral principles. The Pali word "*dhamma*" has multiple meanings, including "creation," "institution," "fairness," "natural," "honesty," and politeness. The word, as it is commonly used in Buddhism, represents the Buddha's teachings

[21] James L. Fitzgerald, "*Dharma* and its Translation in the *Mahābhārata*" in Patrick Olivelle (ed.), *Dharma: Studies in its Semantic, Cultural and Religious History*, Motilal Banarsidass Publishers Private Limited, Delhi, 2009.

and tenets. Since the word "*Dhamma*" means "to uphold," it is essential to Buddhist thought since it both "holds up" the religion and, in the case of Buddhists, the natural order of the cosmos. The term "*Dhamma*" refers to a single concept, which is the Teaching of the Buddha, the truth or natural law he discovered.

2.4 THE KEY PRINCIPLES OF BUDDHISM

Buddhism's basic teachings are the eightfold path, the four noble truths, and the middle way. Buddhism emphasizes the importance of compassion and wisdom being intertwined. Buddha offered workable solutions for everyone's growth, spiritual development and well-being in human society, as well as for compassion and kindness toward all living beings. By promoting the growth of knowledge, empathy, and understanding as well as self-awareness, it seeks to help people live moral lives. The Middle Way is a metaphor for living a moderate life and exercising self-control over one's feelings and actions. If Dana (giving) is meant to be a formal religious act, then the intended audience is a monk or someone who has reached a certain level of spiritual development. Buddhism asserts that it has the capacity to cleanse and change the giver's perspective. Buddhists hold that giving without expecting anything in return can lead to a greater sense of inner strength, long-lasting contentment, and spiritual richness. The *Dhamma,* or teachings of the Buddha, addressed basic issues about the nature of life, the human predicament, and the self. These are all acknowledged philosophical issues in the Western tradition. The Buddha also emphasized the need of upholding moral principles.

The terms "*Dhamma*" (Pāḷi) and "*Dharma*" (Sanskrit) refer to the teachings of the Buddha, which are the truths or natural laws that he discovered, applied to achieve liberation, and imparted to others. Depending on the context, the terms "*dhammā*" or "*dharmā*" might refer to various phenomena, objects, experiences, situations, conditions of being, or realities. The *Dhamma,* also known as *Dharma* in Sanskrit, is a collection of decrees that constituted the policy of Ashoka the Great, the third Mauryan Emperor, who ascended to the Mauryan throne in modern-day India in 269 B.C.E.

Religion, or *Dharma,* is a dimension of reality that changes with time. Every instant is a new dimension of reality that can be realized by playing roles that are appropriate for the moment in order to resolve the dimension of reality in the moment before and reveal the dimension of reality in the moment after. The necessary, conscious state known as *Dhamma* is what enlightens a person to their place in the current reality. By prioritizing its human relationships over the placement of astrological alignments, Sampradaya is the denomination that hinders the momentum growth of the right moment. As a result, every time becomes a good time to take advantage of the ability to reason. When intuition directs suitable conduct, guided by the road of recognizing the potential, the role becomes a variable that changes with time.

When a person is aware of the purpose behind their birth and allows that awareness to direct their appropriate behavior along the road of dedication to that reason, their role in the universe remains constant. One can transcend the cause for the realization of the present, where one's deeds become the reason for one's birth, where the role is defined in terms of the reason. Instead of becoming a reason-taker, a denomination allows one to be the reason-maker.

2.5 JOHN ROSS CARTER'S INTERPRETATION OF *DHAMMA*

Dhamma is a complex and comprehensive term in Theravada Buddhist vocabulary.

2.5.1 Five Traditional Meaning of *Dhamma*

- Guna (quality or Virtue)
- Desanai (Teaching)
- Hetu (cause)
- Pariyatti (Authoritative teaching)
- Nissatta (without a living being) Nissatta-Nijjiva (Lifelessness)
- It can also represents truths, wisdom, merit, vinaya violation and that to be known (heyya)
- Sinhalese sources: it introduced definitions like constitution, condition, object, custom and nibbana[22].

2.6 RUPERT GETHIN'S INTERPRETATION OF *DHAMMA*

Understanding the concept of *Dharma* in early Buddhist literature is the main goal of Rupert Gethin's book He Who Sees Dhmma Sees *Dhammas*: *Dhamma* in Early Buddhism. The primary sources, which are middle indic texts, are found in Pali texts. Since the word "*Dhamma*" is the Pali Middle Indic form, it will be utilized. Magdelene and Wilhelm Geiger's earlier research claim that the approach was used as a thorough philosophical analysis. The focus on the particularly Buddhist technical term "*Dharma*" as a component of existence, as found in literature such as Vasubandhu's AbhiDharmakos' a bhas (fourth and fifth centuries CE), is what Stcherbatsky claims. The method of John Ross Carter, which draws from a wider range

---

22 John Ross Carter, Traditional Definitions of the Term "*Dhamma*" Philosophy East and West, Vol. 26, No. 3 (Jul., 1976), pp. 329–337.

of religious viewpoints and stresses the concept of "*Dhamma*" as a Buddha's teaching, a route for religious practice, and a subject of devotion.[23]

2.6.1 Six Basic Meaning of *Dhamma*

- The teaching of Bhudda
- Good conduct or good behaviour
- The truth
- Nature or quality
- Natural law or order
- A basic mental or physical state or thing

The Buddha's teachings are referred to as *Dhamma*. It includes the lessons he taught and the oral narratives he used to convey them. The *Vinaya, Sutta,* and *Abhidhamma* are the three collections into which these teachings are divided.[24]

Good conduct or Behaviour: The *Dhamma* symbolizes morality and decency. It has to do with rulers and their supposed virtuous or just reign. Possession can be obtained legally or illegally, and *Dhamma* is connected to moral behavior. Practices include the four mindfulness-establishing techniques, the four moral pursuits, the four success-basis, the five faculties, the five powers, the seven awakening factors, and the honorable eight-fold path.

Truth: Truth is symbolized by the *Dhamma*, particularly the realization of the ultimate truth as taught by the Buddha. The Buddha guides his disciples through the process of discovering the reality of suffering, including its cause, source, and means of emancipation. In this context, *Dhamma* refers to the distinct perception of ultimate reality.

Nature: *Dhamma* can also refer to the innate qualities or nature of things. It describes the natural emergence and cessation of things. It is usual in Pali and Sanskrit to use this way.

Natural Law: Some scholars propose that the *Dhamma* is a representation of a natural law or order that governs the cosmos. To enlighten minds, it is perceived as immanent, eternal, uncreated, and comprehensible. The texts support this interpretation more through inference than through explicit language.

Mental or physical state or thing: *Dhamma* can also apply to metal or physical situations or things in a very Buddhistic sense. This is specific to Bhuddhism and is difficult to translate accurately.

---

[23] Rupert Gethin, "He who sees *Dhamma* sees *Dhamma*s: *Dhamma* in Early Buddhism," in *Journal of Indian Philosophy*, Vol. 32, No. 5/6 (December 2004), pp. 513–542.

[24] *Ibid.*

Observing the *Dhamma* **as itself:** The monk observes *Dhamma*s concerning the elements of awakening, aggregates, senses, obstacles, and the noble truths.

2.7 NIKAYAS: USAGES OF *DHAMMA*

This insight goes beyond simple theory to include an understanding of the emergence, persistence, and termination of certain features.

The term *Dhamma*in nikayas is not limited to doctrinal prepositions or teachings. It primarily represents the basic, intrinsic qualities of existence. This wage aligns with the abhidharma perspective.

Understading *Dhamma* in Pali contemporaries: Ranges from 4 to 11 meanings, totalling 18 possible interpretations.

2.7.1 Detailed Exploration of Principle

- Teaching or text: meaning refers to the word of the Buddha
- Good qualities or conduct: involves moral and ethical aspects
- Truth: particularly related to the 4 noble truths
- Natural conditions: signifies the inherent state of something
- Mental or physical quality in Abhidhamma: basic elements of experience

2.7.2 Technical Abhidhamma Understanding

- *Dhamma* as a basic mental or physical quality
- *Dhamma* as sabhava (Particular nature)
- *Dhamma* related to 'not-self' (amatta)
- *Dhamma* as causal conditions (Hetu, Paccaya)
- *Dhamma* as object of consciousness

2.7.3 Transcendent *Dhamma* and Three-fold Division

- Nine transcendent *Dhammas*: includes paths, fruits and Nibhana
- *Dhamma* as knowledge of Nibbana
- *Dhamma* related to doubts about Buddhist texts and realization.

Three fold understanding:

- Text
- Practice
- Attainment

Modern scholars and Natural Law

Commentarial insights align with modern scholarly interpretation.

2.8 THE DEVELOPMENT OF BUDDHIST UNDERSTANDING OF *DHAMMA*

- Originally *Dhamma* had a different meaning in early Buddhist texts
- It evolved its original usage over time
- Plural usage of *Dhamma* (*Dhammas*)
- *Dhammas* refer to the constituents of the world of experience as perceived by the mind
- The embody the law of the world, including the arising disappearance, fleetingness and emptiness of reality.

Interpretation of development of *Dhamma*

- Geigers' view *Dhamma* represents the law of the world or ultimate truth about reality
- Gombrich's view initially, *Dhamma* referred to the teaching of the Buddha and through meditation, individuals began to see the world through these teachings.

Pre-Buddhist usage

- In vedic context, *Dhammaa* referred to practices that maintain and support the cosmic and social order.

Prescription and Descriptive meaning

- *Dhamma* in early Buddhist text has two primary meanings
- Normative and prescriptive refers to practices recommended by the Buddha.
- Descriptive and factual represents the basic qualities that constitute reality.
- Early Indian thought assumed a connection between an entity's nature (*Dharma*) and its prescribed duties (*Dharma*).

According to Rupert Gethin, the term *Dhamma* does not refer only to an irreducible element; it can also refer to mental or physical attributes. Buddhist schools that came after dispute over the ontological and metaphysical character of *Dhammas*. All experience and reality are sustained and upheld by the essential characteristics known as *Dhamma*. Their comprehension of the essence of life is indispensable. English translations of the *Dhamma* are difficult. The translation "quality" is accurate, however it leaves out important details. Its profundity and theological importance may not be adequately conveyed by other translations, such as teaching, legislation, or doctrine.[25]

---

[25] Rupert Gethin, "He who sees *Dhamma* sees *Dhammas*: *Dhamma,* in Early Buddhism" in *Journal of Indian Philosophy*. Vol. 32, No. 5/6 (December 2004) pp. 513–542.

According to Historian Romila Thapar, *Dhamma* is translated as morality, piety, righteousness and so forth. The policy of *Dhamma* was a policy rather of social responsibility than merely of demanding that the entire population should favour Buddhism. It was the building up of an attitude of mind in which social behaviour, the behaviour of one person towards another, was considered of great importance. It was a plea for the recognition of the dignity of man, and for a humanistic spirit in the activities of society. The *Dhamma* of Aśoka emerges as a way of life incorporating a number of ideals and practices. Abstinence from killing was an important principle, as also was the insistence of considerate family relationships and social relationships, whether these were between parents and children, elders and young people, friends, or various ideological sects. The concept of *Dharma* used in the sense of Law and Social Order was by no means new to Mauryan India. Aśoka, with the propagation of his *Dhamma*, made an attempt to humanize it and show that in fact what mattered most was virtuous behaviour. The ability to distinguish between virtuous and unvirtuous behaviour is what distinguishes man from the rest of creation, and the practice of virtue can be made common to all men. The *Dhamma* embodying such behaviour transcends all barriers of sectarian belief. As we have said before, *Dhamma* was largely an ethical concept related to the individual in the context of his society. In the propagation of his *Dhamma* Aśoka was attempting to reform the narrow attitude of religious teaching, to protect the weak against the strong, and to promote throughout the empire a consciousness of social behaviour so broad in its scope, that no cultural group could object to it. Ashoka *Dhamma*'s was in essence an attempt on the part of the king to suggest a way of life which was both practical and convenient, as well as being highly moral. Aśoka was suggesting that a life led according to the principles of his *Dhamma* would bring such a reward for common people.[26]

2.9 THE CONCEPT OF *DHARMA* BY MARGARET CHATTERJEE

Complexity of *Dharma*

In Indian philosophy, *Dharma*, which means righteousness, is a complicated idea. It goes beyond societal, moral, legal, and religious boundaries. Its centuries-long use reflects attempts to strike a balance between institution and ideal, truth and meaning. Being dharmik, or righteous, is a very praiseworthy trait.[27] *Dharma* as an idea has a lengthy history, dating

[26] Romila Thapar, "*Aśoka and the Decline of the Mauryas*, Oxford University Press, New Delhi, 2001, pp. 2–3, pp. 167–181.

[27] Margaret Chatterjee, "The Concept of *Dharma*" in M.C. Doeser and J.N. Kraay (eds.) Facts and Values. Philosophical reflections from Western and Non-Western Perspectives, Martinus Nijhoff Publishers, Dordrecht. 1986, pp. 177–188.

back to the early Vedic era.It began when the Aryans arrived in India approximately 1500 B.C. The original idea was called *Rta*, which stood for both cosmic order and righteousness. The formation of *Dharma* was aided by the writings of the Upanishads, *Brahmanas*, Aranyakas, and Vedas. They included teachings on meditation, the concept of Sanatana-Dharma (external Law), and instructions for making sacrifices. The essence of *Dharma* developed from *Rta* and included right actions, reflecting the way nature operates. It emphasized harmony and balance while acknowledging roles in the home, community, and environment. *Dharma*, together with artha (wealth) and kama (desire), was one of the three guiding principles of life. In conventional hierarchical civilizations, the majority of people lived their lives in accordance with these values. *Dharma* evolved from life stages (asrama-Dharmas) to caste obligations (varma-Dharma). It adjusted to various responsibilities and functions according to a person's station in life (saDharmas). Maintaining societal stability by making sure that everyone has a place and obligations was made possible by *Dharma*. It sought to avert social unrest.[28]

2.10 *DHARMA'S* APPLICATION VARIED THROUGH FOUR STAGES

- Brahmacharya (student life)
- Garhasthya (hosehold)
- Vanaprastha (retreat)
- Sannyasa (renunciation)

Each stage had its own duties and obligations

The emphasis of *Dharma* was on becoming detached from worldly pleasures and belongings. Moksha, which is defined as freedom from the cycle of reincarnation and sorrow, was the ultimate aim. It goes beyond the boundaries of right and wrong. *Dharma* brought up issues with duties that conflicted, as demonstrated in the Mahabharta when Arjun had to choose between his caste obligations and using violence. Certain Indian systems emphasize detachment and permit jiwanmukti, or freedom, within this existence. Karma ruled deeds, and the results dictated what would happen in the future. Samsara, which emphasizes the suffering of humankind, is the term for the cycle of birth, death, and rebirth. As a mediator between the transcendent and the empirical, *Dharma* functioned as a cosmic, individual, and social principle. It brought together the desire of spiritual emancipation (moksha) with ethical regulation. These days, *Dharma* is used to defend social change and criticize accepted conventions. It is still a flexible idea that can be modified and reinterpreted.[29] The epic

[28] *Ibid*

[29] *Ibid*

Mahabharata, particularly the Bhagawad Gita, highlights the complexities of *Dharma*. It explores the tension between, ethics and faith in God.

2.11 DIFFERENT ASPECTS OF HUMAN EXISTENCE

"What is the purpose of Human Existence?" One is having significant and satisfying experiences with being alive. We can say that the knowledge that humans are social beings in addition to physical and psychological ones is the basis of our existence. Put differently, our relationships with other people—significant or not—define who we are and how we live. Existentialists agree that our self-consciousness and ability to exist for ourselves, which entails our freedom and accountability for our actions, are what set humans apart from other living things. The goal of life, according to evolution, is to endure, procreate, and transfer genetic material to the following generation.

Spiritual and Religious views: A lot of spiritual and religious views hold that there is a greater purpose for human life, whether it is to find enlightenment, fulfil a divine design, or acquire moral teachings.

- ♦ Facility enabling
- ♦ Facility embroiling
- ♦ Need for roots
- ♦ Need for branches
- ♦ Temptation to soar
- ♦ Values in everyday life
- ♦ Fire and sun
- ♦ Tapanya (Austerity which sears)

Dharma essentially directs people towards their moral obligations and responsibilities. The conflict between the need for transcendence and the need to be rooted in the realities and moral principles of daily life is highlighted by Chatterjee's comparison. It draws attention to the exterior human struggle to strike a balance between different facets of life.

2.12 ASHOKA'S *DHAMMA*

According to Ashoka, the *Dhamma* compromises several virtues, including truthfulness, compassion, liberality, purity, and a low number of crimes. An attempt is made to distinguish between good and harmful deeds in the third pillar edict. Ashoka thought that people would achieve happiness if they lived their lives in accordance with the *Dhamma*'s policy. The core teachings of Ashoka's *Dhamma* were mutual respect, non-violence, and tolerance for people of different faiths and beliefs. Concern for the welfare of its people was one of the state's priorities. The *Dhamma*'s core principles included kindness, generosity, sincerity, purity, and gentleness. One of the most remarkable figures in Indian history, Emperor Ashok, was a Buddhist convert who devoted his time to spreading *Dhamma*, or "moral principles," as opposed to religion. He mentions the *Dhamma* in his second inscription. It provides an accurate image of his policies and how he views his people as his children. During his rule, Ashoka demonstrated to the country the path towards social, economic, political, and religious progress. He established a norm that is fatherly and grounded on justice. He served as a social justice inspiration. As a result, Ashoka may be regarded as the prophet of societal cohesion and well-being. Additional humanitarian initiatives, such planting trees and drilling wells, were included in the *Dhamma* program. Ashoka denounced ceremonies and sacrifices, deeming them useless. A body of authorities known as *Dhamma* mahamattas was founded in order to put the many parts of *Dhamma* into practice and raise awareness of them. Ashoka assigned them the mission of evangelizing to other sections of society, but in due course they developed into a formidable order of *Dhamma* priests and soon began interfering in political affairs. Romila Thapar says that Ashoka's *Dhamma* is a great documentation of his basic humanism and a reaction to the socio-political needs of his day. It was not anti-Brahmanical, as respect for the Brahmans and Sarmanas is a fundamental aspect of his *Dhamma*. His emphasis on non-violence did not cause him to become indifferent to what the government wanted. In fact, he considered bureaucrats to be in charge of ensuring the moral progress of his citizens.

2.13 ASHOKA'S ROCK EDICTS TABLE

Edict	Ashoka Inscription Details
Major Rock Edict I	Prohibition of animal sacrifice, especially during festive seasons.
Major Rock Edict II	Medical treatment of humans and animals, planting of fruits, medicinal herbs and the digging of wells. Mentions the Pandyas, Satyapuras and Keralaputras of South India.
Major Rock Edict III	Generosity to Brahmins. About Yuktas, Pradeshikas and Rajukas who would go every five years to different parts of his empire to spread *Dhamma*.
Major Rock Edict IV	*Dhammaghosha* (sound of *Dhamma*/righteousness) over Bherighosha (sound of war). The King Ashoka attached greatest value to his duty.
Major Rock Edict V	About *Dhammamahamatras*. Talks about treating slaves right. A special cadre of officials, *Dhamma* Gosha were appointed and entrusted with the duty of spreading *Dhamma* within the kingdom.
Major Rock Edict VI	King's desire to know about his people's conditions. About welfare measures.

Edict	Ashoka Inscription Details
Major Rock Edict VII	Tolerance towards religions among all sects and welfare measures for the public in his as well as his neighbouring kingdoms.
Major Rock Edict VIII	Ashoka's first visit to Bodh Gaya and the Bodhi tree (his first *Dhamma* Yatra). Gave importance to *Dhamma* tours.
Major Rock Edict IX	Condemns popular ceremonies. Stresses on moral conduct.
Major Rock Edict X	Disapproves of the individual's desire for fame and glory and stresses on *Dhamma*.
Major Rock Edict XI	*Dhamma* is the best policy to follow, which includes respect for elders and concern for slaves and servants.
Major Rock Edict XII	It mentions Mahamattas in charge of women's welfare, Ithijika Mahamatta and tolerance towards the *Dhamma* of others.
Major Rock Edict XIII	Mentions victory over Kalinga. Mentions Ashoka's *Dhamma* victory over Greek Kings Antiochus of Syria (Amtiyoko), Ptolemy of Egypt (Turamaye), Magas of Cyrene (Maka), Antigonus of Macedon (Amtikini), Alexander of Epirus (Alikasudaro). Also mentions Pandyas, Cholas, etc. The thirteenth rock edict which was issued at the end of the Kalinga war gives a vivid picture of the change of Ashoka from an aggressive and violent warrior to a great lover and preacher of peace. The direct and immediate effect of the Kalinga war was the conversion of Ashoka to Buddhism.
Major Rock Edict XIV	Purpose of rock edicts.

2.14 *DHARMA* AND *DHAMMA*: COMPARATIVE ANALYSIS (SIMILARITIES AND DIFFERENCES)

They both signify global truth, natural rules, cosmic order, righteousness, feeling of responsibility, and ultimate moral obligation, among other things. Both Buddhism's Nibbana and Hinduism's Moksha aid in achieving salvation. Both refer to a thing's nature or form. In opposition to socio-political structures, both signify the moral and duty obligations of each individual based on their position and role. More similar to a way of life than a religion, *Rajadharma* and *Rajadhamma* are seen as superior to rulers and serve as a governing and directing force for the monarchy or state.

Contrasting *Dharma* and *Dhamma*, the Buddhist *Dhamma* rejects the existence of God, the soul, and divinity, in contrast to Hindu *Dharma*. The *Dhamma* has nothing supernatural about it; rather, it is like cosmic forces and natural laws that uphold nature's order. Unlike Hindu *Dharma*, while Buddhist *Dhamma* is the ultimate moral code founded on the laws of nature and cosmic power, Hindu *Dharma* is seen as a divine edict that transgressors would face divine retribution. The Hindu *Dharma* is not put to the test of reason, logic, or rationality, in contrast to the Buddhist *Dhamma*. As a result, Hindu *Dharma* is more religious, akin to a command from God, but Buddhist *Dhamma* is more like to natural principles that people can understand using reason. Upholding Varna Ashram is not part of Buddhist *Dharma*, and Buddhist kings are not required to maintain Dharma-based social order. While Hindu *Dharma* is seen as a heavenly decree that transgressors will suffer divine vengeance, Buddhist *Dhamma* is the ultimate moral rule based on the laws of nature and cosmic power. Unlike the Buddhist *Dhamma*, the Hindu *Dharma* is not placed to the test of logic, reason, or rationality. Because of this, Buddhist *Dhamma* is more like natural laws that people can comprehend rationally, while Hindu *Dharma* is more religious and resembles an order from God.

In summary, *Dharma* is supreme, sovereign not the king: political obligation only till the king follows raj *Dharma* and upholds *Dharma*. The king in created for the protection of *Dharma* and the world. Using of *Dharma* a king becomes a deity, otherwise he becomes evil. So, a king is the form of *Dharma*. Living in anarchy could be the worst things; hence people should obey laws and king's orders if he is able to maintain peace and order. People can live heavily only if they live under the law and abide by the rules and regulation of the state. King is visible symbol of God on earth, hence people should obey him for peace and as they obey God. At the outset it may be observed that *danda*, dandaniti, arthašāstra, nitišästra, rājajästra, rājanīti and rajadharma are more or less synonyms signifying, in general, the rules of conduct of kings, regulations relating to the production and acquisition of wealth, and ideals of administration which came within the purview of the science of government. The term *danda* appears to have been used in different periods of antiquity for a staff that was meant to ward off demons, who came to disturb a sacrifice, or for driving away cattle, or for signifying the attainment of manhood by a youth on the completion of his initiation (upanayanam), or for the handle of a ladle, or a similar implement used in a sacrifice, or, as in most cases, for a weapon.

MODEL QUESTIONS FOR PRACTICE

2.1 Explain the concept of *Dharma* in Ancient Indian Traditions.

2.2 Describe the similarities and differences between '*Dharma* and *Dhamma*'.

2.3 '*Dharma* and *Danda* are two pillars of the Hindu Conception of State'. Do you agree? Substantiate your answer with suitable examples.

2.4 Explain the concept and meaning of Ashoka's *Dhamma*.

2.5 Explain the concept of *Dharma, Dhamma* and *Danda* in Indian Political thought.

2.6 Differentiate the concept of *Dharma* and *Dhamma* in Ancient Indian history.

2.7 Discuss the different meanings and ideas conveyed by *'Dharma'* in the ancient Indian Political Thoughts.

2.8 Explain the meanings and ideas conveyed by *'Dhamma'* in Buddhist Political Thought.

2.9 Ancient Indian Polity was interplay of *Dharma* and *Danda*. Discuss.

2.10 Discuss the different meanings and ideas conveyed by *'Danda'* in the ancient Indian Political Thoughts.

2.11 *Danda* is the soul of *Dharma*; discuss the inter-relationship between *Dharma* and *Danda* in the light of this statement.

3

Danda

3.1 MEANING OF DANDA IN ANCIENT INDIA

Danda is a set of rules that God gave humanity to live with moral values. As per the Vāstusūtra Upaniṣad, daṇḍa is listed as a weapon. Punishment, or dada, is essential to society's upkeep of harmony and law. Danda is a compound word that means "to restrain" (Dama). A person is restrained from misbehavior by the use of danda. The monarch is known as Danda-Dhar in ancient Indian Polity. Danda is seen as a fundamental characteristic of kingship.

The term "Danda" has various meanings and connotations, including "religious stick," "punishment," "just use of force," "state's will and authority," "dispensation of justice," "realized justice" (Nyaya), "administration of state—statecraft," and "science of politics." Fear of punishment maintains peace and order, as people only engage in lawful activities out of fear of being punished by the king, who was in charge of punishing them and was created to correct human vices and restrain them in order to guide them toward a fulfilling life.

3.2 DANDA OR CONCEPT OF PUNISHMENT MENTIONED IN DIFFERENT DOCUMENTS

According to Manusmriti, "Punishment have been prescribed by the sages, so that righteousness may not be outraged and unrighteousness may be cured". The whole world is rectified by Danda and even the Gods and Demi-Gods are subject to authority. In Kautilya's Arthashastra Danda as an instrument for bringing people under control, maintain peace and order. Danda is a part of the four-fold policy of the State—"Sama, Dama, Danda and Bheda".

According to the Puranas, punishment purifies sin in the same way as medicine heals the guilty. According to Sukra-Niti, punishment is the ultimate "stay of virtue" since it drives out immoral behavior and social evil. According to Kamandaka, punishment is appropriate when it serves justice. According to Yajnavalkya Smriti, punishment should set the guilty on the correct course. According to Sage Gautam, the purpose of punishment was to identify wrongdoers and miscreants.

3.3 DANDA: ADMINISTRATION OF JUSTICE

Danda represented the state's will, legitimacy, monopoly on the use of force, and legal authority over violence. It represented the state's sovereignty in a sense. Using the Danda was the only method to maintain social order and peace in the state. The Danda is attributed to the creator of the universe, Prajapati. The proper application of the Danda was the assurance of world peace, happiness, and justice. Danda is intended to cleanse the transgressor, atone for human misdeeds, and provide respite from society's miseries.

Danda guards and rules; Danda preserves Dharma, Artha, and Kāma. Danda guided everyone and assisted men in making moral decisions. It stands for the scientific study of statecraft, politics, governance, and estate upkeep. Dharma's soul is called Danda, and Dharma is the actual law.

Danda helped men make moral decisions by acting as a mentor to all of them. Within the context of ancient Indian philosophy and governance, the term "danda" signifies authority, control, or retribution. Its significance is in maintaining justice and order, even though interpretations vary across cultures and historical eras. It represents the science of politics, management, statecraft, and estate maintenance. Danda is the core of Dharma; it is the means by which Dharma was justly applied.

Danda is also referred to as the soul of Dharma. "To restrain" is derived from the Arabic word "Dama." It is not permitted to act inappropriately. One specific explanation for Danda's religious tinge is that it gives them legitimacy or authority. Danda stood for everyone's pleasure and fairness. Dand-Dhar was the name of the king in ancient Indian politics. Danda is seen as a prerequisite for royalty.

3.4 DANDANITI

Dandaniti is the art and science of politics, statecraft, force of administration, and government. Dandaniti was given by God to King in order to provide equal justice to all members of the society, promote peace, progress, and prosperity among the populace, safeguard the state's welfare, ensure effective administration, defend the weaker from the stronger, punish the offender, and ultimately maintain everyone within the bounds of dharma."

It is only through Danda that the king can manage the affairs of the State and can guide everyone to be on the path of Dharma; following dandaniti to maintain peace, order and bring prosperity happiness and welfare to people is his highest duty. It is a mechanism to destroy evil as the sun destroys the darkness. If the Dandaniti is destroyed, essence of dharma will be destroyed leading to anarchy; everything will be eclipsed by darkness. When everyone else is asleep, Danda and the fear of Danda are the ones that are awake, and in the end, the concept of Danda is what controls everyone's behavior in the society. Danda uphold Dharma: one refrains from engaging in sinful activities out of fear of Danda. Dandaniti denote dispensation of justice—punishment to evil, reward to righteous/ virtous; it also denote relation of individual to the state, totality of social, political and economic relationship and structure and functioning of the state.

First recorded by Usanasa, the term "Dandniti" is mentioned in the Mahabharata in reference to the "Book 'Dandniti' attributed to Prajapati." Prajapati is credited with creating the danda. The god Shiva worked hard to create the Danda, which serves as the foundation for even the Science of Politics.

3.5 DONALD R. DAVIS JR.'S INTERPRETATION ON DANDA

The practical means by which the law is applied and enforced is punishment. In practical terms, it is essential to the application of legal principles. Certain routes allow dharma, or morality, to enter the field of practice. As an indirect route, the Vedas and their uninterrupted transmission through learned traditions are used.

Broad responsibilities of the ruler

The ruler's responsibilities extend beyond following the law overnight. The duties of the monarch are highly valued in Hindu law, particularly when it comes to safeguarding the populace and maintaining the caste system and life stages.

The foundation of the method for achieving societal advancement and protection is punishment. It is regarded as essential to preserving and enhancing social order. The Hindu law code goes into great depth regarding the penalties for various offenses. These writings were essential tools for comprehending the Hindu legal theory of punishment.

The Danda as a means of monitoring violations

Dana serves as a check on numerous dharma infractions committed by people. Hindu legal doctrine frequently personifies punishment as a deity, highlighting the deity's function as a defender of dharma.[1]

---

[1] Donald R. Davis Jr, "Rectitude and Rehabilitation (danda) in The Spirit of Hindu Law", Cambridge University Press, NY, 2010, pp. 128–143.

Dandaniti: Art and science of governance, administration of force

It can be defined as compulsion, punishment, a fine, the reasonable use of force, or just plain justice depending on the situation. It was implemented for the welfare of the state; for the equitable administration of justice to all members of society; for the advancement and prosperity of the populace; for the protection of the weaker against the stronger; for the punishment of the transgressor; and, lastly, for the maintenance of everyone within the bounds of Dharma.

The king can only run the state's affairs and direct everyone toward the path of dharma through danda. The king can guarantee the happiness and well-being of the populace by adhering to dandaniti, which upholds peace, order, and prosperity. It is a system to eliminate evil in the same way that light eliminates darkness. Everyone in the community is subject to behavioral regulations based on the concept of danda.

The danda was a crucial component of ancient Indian governance. Lord Shiva was the one who created Danda. We could refer to it as a "politics science" that was developed using Danda. Dharma itself is Danda; it is the soul of Dharma. The danda principle is infinitely powerful. The Danda is the legitimate authority that embodies the will of the state. As such, it possesses both legal and moral precedence. It is the cornerstone of the social being. Danda was the promise of justice and happiness for everybody.

The two roles that the legendary idea of Danda fulfilled were protection and governance. Manu is of the same opinion regarding danda. Dharma, artha, and kama are governed by danda. Danda is a purifying method[2]. Kautliya views danda as a tool for controlling individuals. In ancient Indian politics, the king was referred to as danda dhar. Danda had a strong connection to metaphysics and theology. It was seen as the authority that carried out the wishes of the state. Danda was viewed as a way to purify the state as well as the individual. Danda was associated with the government, and officers were in charge of carrying it out.

It was thought that danda was necessary to uphold social order, universal happiness, and righteousness since he corrected human vices and guided society in the correct direction. Danda was viewed as a tool for checking miscreants and wrongdoers; it contained both reformatory and retributive elements, with the goal of purifying the offender.

3.6 FORMS OF DANDA

In simple terms danda is an ancient symbol of authority. It speaks of the application of force and punishment to uphold political objectives and

[2] Radha Krishna Choudhary, "Theory of Punishment in Ancient India", in Proceedings of the Indian History Congress, Vol. 10, 1947, pp. 166–171.

preserve order. In addition to seizing and holding onto power, Danda Niti seeks to ensure that the populace receives benefits and resources in an equitable manner.

- Warning
- Censure
- Fine
- Corporal punishment
- The deterrence and education of both sin and crime

3.7 DANDA'S CHARACTERISTICS

In a sense, the term "Danda" defined the sovereignty of the state and represented the will, authority, coercive power, and lawful monopoly of violence of the state. The state and society were only able to maintain peace and order through the use of the Danda. The Danda is said to have been created by Prajapati, the creator of the universe. Universal peace, happiness, and righteousness were guaranteed by the proper application of the Danda. The purpose of Danda is to atone for human vices, cleanse the offender, and escape the horrors of societal order. Danda rules, guards preserves Kama, Artha, and Dharma. Danda served as a mentor to everyone and assisted men in making moral decisions. It stands for the science of politics, statecraft, administration, and estate maintenance. Dharma is the essence of Dharma. Dharma was truly applied justly through the use of Danda and only righteous and just rulers, not despots and corrupt ones, can hold Danda.

3.8 THEORY OF PUNISHMENT

"Punishment has been prescribed by the ages so that righteousness may not be outraged and unrighteousness may be cured".[3] The ancient Indian theory of punishment was based on the central idea that punishment for wrong-doing was to be meted out by the king for the preservation of social order.[4]

In ancient Indian law, punishment described that it should help the man or the criminal to reform himself according to the prescribed codes of Dharma.

Punishment was fixed with accuracy and those who violated the king's peace or justice were heavily punished after being duly examined by the court.

---

[3] Radha Krishna Choudhary, "Theory of Punishment in Ancient India", *In*: Proceedings of the Indian History Congress, Vol. 10, 1947, pp. 166–171.

[4] *Ibid*

Punishment is a basic power, which is a means of supremacy of law, which should be used by the king not on his own will but keeping in mind the basis and purpose, because the use of punishment for selfish reasons can destroy the state itself.

Therefore, punishment should be used after analyzing various aspects, because punishment given due to partiality, selfishness, accumulation of power and greed, etc. is such a 'vicious punishment' which leads to revolution in the society. Therefore, only punishment combined with law helps the king and the people in achieving the real justice (Trivarga). Therefore, the ultimate goal of man has been expressed by linking punishment and religion with power and purpose respectively.

According to Kautilya, Dandaniti is the policy which helps in achieving the desired goal. It helps in protecting the achieved meaning and helps in increasing the protected meaning. In this way the whole world is under its control. Kautilya has also written about the ancient Vedic sage Ushna that he considered Dandaniti as the only knowledge and according to him, the proper planning of Trivarga is implemented through this. It is only through this that man can follow the proper system of religion, wealth and work.[5]

3.9 PREVENTIVE PUNISHMENTS IN ANCIENT TIMES

3.9.1 Preventive Punishment System

This punishment was used to control crime, that is, under the penal system, punishment was determined by giving warning in advance, so that crime would not be committed in future due to fear of punishment. Kautilya paid special attention to this system, because according to him, fear and terror in themselves are effective measures to prevent crime. These punishments were given in open places, so that the fear of that punishment remains among the public, such as physical punishment. Examples of such punishments included burning the offenders alive, piercing their tongues, tying their hands and feet and hanging them upside down, and pricking their nails with needles.

3.9.2 Corrective Punishment System

Under this system, attention is paid to the rights of both the victim and the criminal for the social welfare, because the function of punishment is to develop welfare in the society and this welfare cannot be achieved only by giving physical punishment. Rather, by examining the mental state of the

---

[5] Radha Krishna Choudhary, "Theory of Punishment in Ancient India", *In*: Proceedings of the Indian History Congress, Vol. 10, 1947, pp. 166–171.

criminal, his mental state is ascertained and he is motivated towards not committing crime, so that he follows the right path. Mahabharata, Kautilya and other religious scriptures have also prescribed this penal policy.

3.9.3 Symbolic Punishment System

The punishment system was based on the feeling of revenge. If a human being caused harm to any part of the body, the same body part was also punished, like eye for eye, hand for hand, etc. That is, the criminal was punished according to his crime. Aaptadosham Karmakarayet, although this punishment system was used more in the early society. Kautilya also supports this penal system and says that the criminal should be punished according to the extent of the crime he has committed, after the crime is proven. Every social and political organization must have some laws or authority without which the human society cannot function.

3.9.4 Retribution and Exploitation Punishments

Punishment had retributive aspects, often seen as a form of divine judgement.

Expiation was used as a way to purify sin and was connected to religious and metaphysical beliefs.

3.9.5 Restraint and Reform Punishments

Various thinkers like Kautilya and Sukra saw punishment as a means to reform criminals. Punishment was considered a way to educate people and instill discipline.

3.9.6 Proportionate Punishment

Punishment was believed to be most effective when proportionate to the crime committed.

3.10 DONALD R. DAVIS JR.'S INTERPRETATION ON PUNISHMENT

- Punishment as law enforcer
- Punishment is the practical instrument for enforcing and applying the law. It plays a pivotal role in bringing legal principles into practical existence.[6]

---

[6] Donald R. Davis Jr., "Rectitude and Rehabilitation (Danda) in the spirit of Hindu Law", Cambridge University Press, NY, 2010, pp. 128–143.

Dharma's introduction into practice

- Dharma, the moral code, enters the realm of practice through specific channels. The Vedas and their unbroken transmission through learned traditions serve as indirect pathway.

Broad responsibilities of the ruler

- The ruler's role goes beyond mere overnight of legal procedures.
- Hindu law places significance importance on the ruler's duties, especially in protecting the people and upholding the caste system and life-stage.

Punishment in Hindu Law

- Punishment is a part of the dharma ritual, balancing inequalities and instilling fear.
- It corrects errors, rehabilitates and educates individuals about their roles in society.
- Punishment is both rehabilitative and ritually efficacious, guiding individuals through the ritual of law.

Punishment as root and means

- Punishment is both the root and the means to achieve the protection and promotion of society.
- It's considered indispensable for safeguarding and advancing societal order.

Elaboration of punishment

- Hindu legal text provides comprehensive detail about punishments for specific crimes. These texts were serving as critical resources for understanding the Hindu legal view of punishment.
- In Hindu jurisprudence, punishment is given often personified as a deity, emphasizing its role as a guardian of dharma.

Punishment in criminal cases is systematically categorized into 6 distinct headings:

- Murder, theft, rape, slander, assault and miscellaneous each with its own specific punishment.
- A plethora of circumstantial factors significantly impacts the determination and administration of punishment.
- Factors like the offenders' caste, nature of the offence, quantity involved and other considerations must be weighed in each case.
- Severity of legal infractions
- Hindu law distinguishes the severity of various legal infractions.
- Aggravated theft, particularly robbery, is considered the most serious offense in Hindu jurisprudence.

- The miscellaneous title within Hindu law serves as a flexible framework. It encompasses a wide range of penal and criminal laws, offering a platform to address various types of violations and disputes.

Rule's active role in penal administration

- The ruler has the authority to initiate investigations and administer punishment for specific crimes. This includes offences against his decrees and violations of state actions, providing an active role in maintain order.

Role of karma

- The concept of karma, which focuses on cosmic moral causation, is relatively unimportant in Hindu laws.

Karma and Dharma relationship

- Karma's consequences do not directly affect the central aspect of dharma (law).
- Dharma is about positive duties and restraints.
- Karma's consequences are a backdrop but do not influence the systematic presentation of dharma regarding castes and life-stages.
- Karma consequences (karmavipaka) are not central to Hindu law but are discussed in detail to encourage adherence to dharma.
- Hindu law emphasizes the role of punishment in prevention and deterrence, not retribution.
- Legal procedures and punishments check criminals, and prevent them from committing further offences.

Maintenance of social order

- Deterrence is essential for maintain social order and personal restraint, which is integral to the functioning of the legal system.

Positive role of punishment

- Punishment in Hindu law has a positive character supporting and making possible the function of the system of castes and life stages.
- It fosters deterrence by promoting rectitude and adherence to dharma. Punishment serves to prevent future normative transgressions and promote lawfulness. Procedural and substantive law mutually reinforce each other in the prevention and correction of legal violations.
- Punishment acknowledges human imperfection and the need to address deviation from an ideal path.
- Law depends on punishment to correct human failings and maintain order.

- Punishment ensures system stability and the reintegration of transgressors.

In summary we can say that, both perspectives highlighted the close connection between law, violence and punishment. Violence and punishment are tools to uphold the legal system, with a focus on deterrence and rehabilitation.

Functions of Danda:

- Danda represented the state's will, authority, coercive power, legitimate monopoly of violence.
- In a sense, it denoted the state's sovereignty.
- Only through the instrument of Danda, peace and order was maintained in society/state.
- **Divine Sanctity:** Prajapati, the creator of the universe, is considered to be the creator of the Danda.
- Just application of Danda was the guarantee of universal peace, happiness and righteousness.
- Danda is designed to correct human vices, purify the sinner, flee the evils from social order.
- Danda protects and and governs; Danda saves Dharma, Artha, and Kāma.
- Danda acted as a guide for all and helped men choose between right and wrong.

Categorization of punishment

Punishment in criminal cases is systematically categorized into 6 distinct headings:

- Murder, theft, rape, slander, assault and miscellaneous each with its own specific punishment.

Circumstantial factors in punishment

- A plethora of circumstantial factors significantly impacts the determination and administration of punishment.
- Factors like the offenders's caste, nature of the offence, quantity involved and other considerations must be weighed in each case.

Severity of legal infractions

- Hindu law distinguishes the severity of various legal infractions.
- Aggravated theft, particularly robbery, is considered the most serious offense in Hindu jurisprudence.

The miscellaneous title within Hindu law serves as a flexible framework. It encompasses a wide range of penal and criminal laws, offering a platform to address various types of violations and disputes.

Ruler's active role in penal administration

The ruler has the power to launch investigations and impose penalties for particular offenses. This involves disobeying his orders and going against the government's rules, actively contributing to the preservation of order.

Two forms of punishment

- **Danda:** This form of punishment involved punishment imposed by legal authority, typically rulers, for both criminal and civil offences.
- **Prayascitta:** It denotes self-imposed penances or expiations for legal or religious transgressions. It is voluntary and depends on the contribution of the offender.

Karma and dharma relationship

- Karma's consequences do not directly affect the central aspect of dharma (law).
- Dharma is about positive duties and restraints.
- Karma's consequences are a backdrop but do not influence the systematic presentation of dharma regarding castes and life-stages.
- Karma consequences (karmavipaka) are not central to Hindu law but are discussed in detail to encourage adherence to dharma.

Retribution and punishment

Prevention and deterrence: Hindu law emphasizes the role of punishment in prevention and deterrence, not retribution.

Maintenance of social order: Deterrence is essential to maintain social order and personal restraint, which is integral to the functioning of the legal system.

Positive role of punishment: Punishment in Hindu law has a positive character supporting and making possible the function of the system of castes and life stages.

It fosters deterrence by promoting rectitude and adherence to dharma. Punishment serves to prevent future normative transgressions and promote lawfulness. Procedural and substantive law mutually reinforce each other in the prevention and correction of legal violations.

Punishment as laws' vehicle

Introduction: Punishment acknowledges human imperfection and the need to address deviation from an ideal path.

Law depends on punishment to correct human failings and maintain order. Punishment ensures system stability and the reintegration of transgressors.

Benjamin's perspective

Benjamin's critique of violence explores the link between violence and law. Violence serves either as a means of law making or law preservation.

Benjamin proposes a revolutionary, non-violent approach to break the cycle of violence in law.

Sarkar's perspective

Sarkar discusses Hindu statecraft, where punishment plays a critical role. In Hindu theory, punishment is educative and maintains the state's order. The state's ability to coerce and restain is central existence.

Common ground

Both perspectives highlighted the close connection between law, violence and punishment.

Violence and punishment are tools to uphold the legal system, with a focus on deterrence and rehabilitation.[7]

MODEL QUESTIONS FOR PRACTICE

3.1 Discuss the different meanings and ideas conveyed by 'Danda' in the Ancient Indian Political Thoughts.

3.2 Danda is the soul of Dharma; discuss the inter-relationship between Dharma and Danda in the light of this statement.

3.3 What is the theory of Punishment in Ancient India?

3.4 Please explain Rectitude and Rehabilitation (Danda) in the spirit of Hindu Law, as per Interpretation given by Donald R. Davis Jr.

[7] Radha Krishna Choudhry, "Theory of Punishment in Ancient India" *In*: Proceedings of the Indian History Congress, Vol. 10, 1947, pp. 166–171.

4

Nyaya and Niti

4.1 NYĀYA: AN INTRODUCTION

There was neither non-existence nor existence then; there was neither the realm of space nor the sky which is beyond. What stirred? Where? In whose protection? Was there water, bottomlessly deep? There was neither death nor immortality then. There was no distinguishing sign of night nor of day. That one breathed, windless, by its own impulse. There were seed-placers; there were powers. There was impulse beneath; there was giving-forth above. Who really knows? Who will here proclaim it? Whence was it produced? Whence is this creation? The gods came afterwards, with the creation of this universe. Who then knows whence it has arisen? Whence this creation has arisen—perhaps it formed itself, or perhaps it did not—the one who looks down on it, in the highest heaven, only he knows—or perhaps he does not know.[1] (*Nāsadīya Sūkta*, Rigveda 10.129)

The above verse is the *Nāsadīya Sūkta*, an excerpt from the Rigveda which is considered to be one of the earliest attempts to *logically* reflect on the beginnings of the Universe. Commonly known as the Creation hymn, the *Nāsadīya Sūkta* acknowledges the difficulty in explaining the origins of existence and in further verses try to explain logically and reasonably the origins of the world. The *sūkta* represents the oldest Indian instance of what is understood as epistemology in western thought; epistemology is a branch of philosophy that concerns itself with the theory of knowledge. Some key epistemological questions are concerned with issues like "what is knowledge?" "what are the sources of our knowledge?" "what do we

[1] Kenneth Kramer, *World Scriptures: An Introduction to Comparative Religions*, Paulist Press, New York, 1986, p. 37.

know?" and "what differentiates knowledge from wisdom and opinion?"[2] It is the human intellectual engagement with understanding the nature of reality and in the process identifying the various methods of knowing and comprehending reality. In the Indian context a separate branch of philosophy dedicated to the understanding of reality is known as *nyāya*. The *Nyāya* derives its name from "*nyāya*," meaning the rules of logical thinking and the means of determining the right thing. Thus, originally indicated as a system of logic, laying down the rules of logical argumentation, *Nyāya*, also known as ānvīkṣiki," blossomed into a systematic school and found its legitimate place among the six Vedic systems of philosophy.[3] The *nyāya* system of Indian philosophy attempts to arrive at *correct* knowledge by eliminating the possibilities of *false* knowledge and several methods are recommended by the scholars of the *Nyāya* School of philosophy for the goal of reaching correct knowledge.

4.2 DARŚANA: INDIAN PHILOSOPHY

Indian philosophy or traditional Indian systems of thoughts incorporates elaborate and highly sophisticated doctrinal and metaphysical discussions and debates among a diverse array of scholars and schools of thoughts. *Darśana* is generally translated as *philosophy* due to its intrinsic similarities with modern western philosophy; however, traditional Indian thinking goes far beyond the confines of western philosophy. Alternatively, the term *theology* is often used to convey the traditional thoughts in Hinduism, which is again an incomplete description. Many of the schools are atheistic and is not concerned with God. *Darśana*, which is derived from verb root *dṛś*, 'to see' implies a 'view' or 'vision' of the world is used to refer to both the *āstika* (orthodox) and *nāstika* (heterodox) belief systems. Āstika or the orthodox system of thought acknowledges the Vedic revelation and the existence of a Self or Brahman. Āstika schools of Indian philosophies include Nyāyá, Vaiśeṣika, Sāṃkhya, Yoga, Mīmāṃsā, and Vedānta. By contrast, the *nāstika* or heterodox system denies the existence of Self or Soul or Brahman. The *nāstika* school of Indian philosophy includes Buddhism, Jainism, Cārvaka and Ājīvika.

Darśanas have codified their teachings in aphorisms or *sūtras* (threads) which are often too condensed to be understood without the use of commentary (*bhāṣya*).[4] It is often suggested that debates and organized

---

2 Koemhong Sol, "Understanding epistemology and its key approaches in research," *Cambodian Journal of Educational Research* (2022), Vol. 2, No. 2, pp. 80–99.

3 Bina Gupta, *An Introduction to Indian Philosophy Perspectives on Reality, Knowledge, and Freedom,* Routledge, New York, 2012, p. 171.

4 Gavin Flood, *Introduction to Hinduism,* Cambridge university Press, 1996, pp. 224–225.

argumentation pervaded Indian philosophical scene and the commentarial literature form exegetical, interpretative and explanatory texts on the fundamental texts of every school of thought. It is in the commentarial literature that refined debates and technical refutations are found. In order to debate on issues, the *darśanas* developed a common terminology, particularly regarding the six means of acquiring valid knowledge (*pramāṇa*): namely perception (*pratyakṣa*), inference (*anumāna*), verbal authority (*śabda*), analogy (*upamāna*), presumption (*arthāpatti*) and non-apprehension (*abhāva*). The different *darśanas* accepted all or some of these means of knowledge.[5]

4.3 UNDERSTANDING NYĀYA

Among the six **āstika** schools of Indian philosophy, *nyāya* is considered one of the most prominent and was based on argumentation and a system which was predominantly intellectual, analytic, logical and epistemological. *Nyāya* is also called *Tarkashāstra* or the science of reasoning; *Pramānashāstra* or the science of logic and epistemology; *Hetuvidyā* or the science of causes; *Vādavidyā* or the science of debate; and *Ānvīksikī* or the science of critical study.[6] Out of the six means of valid knowledge discussed above, *nyāya* recognized four means of gaining valid knowledge (*pramāna*) and the objects of knowledge (*prameya*) in order to arrive at correct knowledge (*tattvajñāna*). From correct knowledge one attains the highest good (*nihśreyasa*). The elimination of false knowledge leads to absolute liberation (*apavarga*) from suffering (*duhkha*) and its causes.[7]

The *Nyāya* was first systematized by Gautama, also known as "Akṣapāda," in the *Nyāya Sūtras* (250–450 CE). The long tradition of commentaries on the *Nyāya Sūtras* of Gautama exists with Vātsyāyana's commentary called *Nyāyabhāṣya* (5th century CE) being the first and then continued by Udyotakara in his *Nyāya vārttika* (7th century CE). Vācaspati commented on *Nyāya vārttika* in his *Nyāya vārttika tīka*.

Let us now understand primary thoughts of the *Nyāya* school as founded by Gautama and continued by his commentators. The following are the fundamental ideas:

1. What we are directly aware of in our perception is the physical reality that exists independently of our awareness of it.
2. We see as well as touch physical objects, wholes, bodies, and their properties as well. But we see and touch wholes and substrata because they have parts and properties, but not necessarily because

---

5 *Ibid*, p. 225.

6 Chandradhar Sharma, *A Critical Survey of Indian Philosophy*, Motilal Banarsidass, Delhi, p. 179.

7 Peter M. Scharf, "The Denotation of Generic Terms in Ancient Indian Philosophy: Grammar, Nyāya, and Mīmāṃsā", *Transactions of the American Philosophical Society*, 1996, New Series, Vol. 86, No. 3 (1996), p. 151.

we see or touch these parts and properties. On the other hand, we do not, in the same sense, smell the flower, but only its fragrance, nor taste the sugar, but taste only its sweetness. Likewise, we do not hear the train, but only its whistle.

3. The whole is a distinct reality, created by the putting together of the parts, and yet distinct from those parts taken together. A substratum is likewise distinct from the properties it instantiates or the property-instantiations it contains.
4. Perceiving or seeing—that is knowing in the most direct sense, and there is no further basis or foundation or ground which is more indubitable or certain and from which such perceptual knowledge is derived or inferred.
5. This knowledge is not always verbalized, but it is verbalizable.
6. An analysis of perceptual illusion is possible without the assumption of sense-data or sense-impressions intervening between the perceiver and the physical world.
7. Ordinary knowledge is neither self-revealing nor self-validating. A cognitive event may occur and pass away unnoticed or unperceived. We can neither recall it nor communicate it to others by using language unless we have first inwardly perceived it. This inward perceiving is called *anuvyavasāya* (inward perception). It is similar to our perception of pain or pleasure.[8]

Nyāya is allied to the *Vaiśeṣika* system. The former develops logic and epistemology whereas the latter develops metaphysics or ontology. One deals with the right knowledge of reality and the other takes up the exposition of reality. *Nyāya* adopts mostly the *Vaiśeşika* metaphysics. So it is called the system of atomistic pluralism and logical realism. Both the systems view the earthly life as full of suffering and they regard liberation as the absolute cessation of suffering. Both agree that bondage is due to ignorance of reality and liberation consists in the right knowledge of reality. However there are some important points of difference between the two schools. Firstly the *Vaiśeṣika* recognizes only seven categories whereas *Nyāya* accepts sixteen categories and includes all the seven of the former in the category called *Prameya* or the knowable. Secondly, the *Vaiśeṣika* admits of only two *Pramanas*, namely, perception and Inference, whereas the Nyāya accepts the four Pramanas, namely, perception, inference, comparison and verbal authority.[9]

---

[8] Bimal Krishna Matilal, *Perception: An Essay on Classical Indian Theories of Knowledge*, Clarendon Press, 1986, pp. 5–6.

[9] Chandradhar Sharma, *A Critical Survey of Indian Philosophy*, Motilal Banarsidass, Delhi, pp. 179–180.

4.4 FUNDAMENTALS OF NYĀYA

Knowledge (*jnāna*) or cognition (*buddhi*) is defined as apprehension (*upalabdhi*) or consciousness (*anubhava*). *Nyāya* believes that knowledge is the revealer of both the subject and the object which are quite distinct from itself. All knowledge is a revelation or manifestation of objects (*arthaprakāsho buddhih*). Just as a lamp manifests physical things placed before it, so knowledge reveals all objects which come before it. Knowledge may be valid or invalid. Valid knowledge (*pramā*) is defined as the right apprehension of an object (*yathārthānubhavah*). It is the manifestation of an object as it is. *Nyāya* maintains the theory of correspondence (*paratali prāinānya*). Knowledge, in order to be valid, must correspond to reality. Valid knowledge is produced by the four valid means of knowledge—perception, inference, comparison and testimony. Invalid knowledge includes memory (*smṛti*), doubt (*samshaya*), error (*viparyaya*) and hypothetical reasoning (*tarka*).[10]

The first *sūtra* of Gautama's *Nyāya* Sūtra, sixteen entities is mentioned. They are as follows[11]:

1. *Pramāṇa* or the means of knowledge
2. *Prameya* or the objects of right knowledge
3. *Samśaya* or doubt
4. *Prayojana* or purpose
5. *Dṛṣtānta* or example (required in inference)
6. *Siddhānta* or conclusion,
7. *Avayava* or components of an inference
8. *Tarka* or counterfactual argument
9. *Nirṇaya*
10. *Vāda*
11. *Jalpa*
12. *Vitaṇḍā*
13. *Hetvābhāsas*
14. *Chala*
15. *Jāti*
16. *Nigrahasthāna*

4.4.1 *Pramāṇa*

A *pramāṇa* is an unfailing method or means of knowing a desired object. *Pramāṇa* accurately represents the object and an object is impossible to

---

[10] *Ibid, p. 180.*

[11] Bina Gupta, *An Introduction to Indian Philosophy Perspectives on Reality, Knowledge, and Freedom,* Routledge, New York, 2012, p. 172.

determine without *pramāṇa*. There are three aspects which are inseparably linked to an object—*knower of the object; the object of knowledge; knowledge itself*. There are four methods or means of knowing (*pramāṇa*):

(i) *Pratyakṣa* (Perception)
(ii) *Anumāna* (Inference)
(iii) *Upamāna* (Comparison)
(iv) *Śabda* (Verbal Testimony)

Let us discuss the four means of knowing in the following subsection:

(i) *Pratyakṣa* (Perception): Etymologically, the meaning of *pratyakṣa* is to be "present before the eyes or any other sense organs," It relates to direct knowledge through sense organs. The *Nyāya* theory defines *pratyakṣa* as a form of valid knowledge which is caused by sense stimulation. Perception is always of an object and according to Gautama's *Nyāya Sūtra*, there are three kinds of objects: the physical objects (e.g., table or chair), specific objects (e.g., color, hard, soft), and internal objects (e.g. pleasure and pain). The *Nyāya Sūtra* also specifies that objects are not linguistic (*avyapadeśa*) which means that object is not infused with meaning by itself, neither is it definite (*vyavasāyātmaka*). Rather, *pratyakṣa* is that cognition which is generated by the self, the sense organs, the mind and a specific contact between them.[12]

(ii) *Anumāna* (Inference): *Anumāna* nearly translates into the term 'inference' in English. The notion of *anumāna* or inference is one of the most interesting aspects of the *Nyāya* School of thought. Inference as a means or mode of knowing is *anumāna* while the inferential cognition is known as *anumiti*. Inference or *anumāna* is that knowledge which arises after (*anu*) another knowledge. Therefore, the knowledge gained through *anumāna* presupposes a prior knowledge. In other words, a cognition emerging through some other cognition is *anumāna*. Hence, *anumāna* is an indirect method of knowing (as opposed to direct knowledge gained through sensory stimulation). The famous instance of inference or *anumāna* is seeing smoke in a distant hill and inferring that there is fire on the hill.[13]

(iii) *Upamāna* (Comparison): Etymologically, *Upamāna* is derived from *upa* meaning similarity and *māna* meaning knowledge or cognition. *Upamāna*, therefore means the knowledge gained through similarity or comparison. In the pramāṇa theory, it is considered a method of attaining valid knowledge. *Upamāna* is the knowledge derived by comparing two objects which may be produced by the knowledge of the similarity or resemblance. The knowledge thus gained through *upamāna* is called *upamiti*. For example, a wild cow in the forest may be recognized as a cow and be

[12] *Ibid*, p. 174.
[13] *Ibid*, p. 177.

identified as a cow because of its similarity with a domesticated cow. This type of knowledge is produced by a prior knowledge of a similar object. Knowledge by *upamāna* is not produced by perception or inference but only by comparison.[14]

(iv) *Śabda* (Verbal Testimony): The fourth means of attaining valid knowledge, according to *Nyāya* is Śabda or verbal testimony. However, it is important to note that śabda or verbal testimony of every human being is not considered a valid means of knowledge. The *Nyāya* doctrine is clear that the statement of only a trustworthy or an authoritative person is considered valid. The term used for trustworthy verbal testimony is *āptavacana. Nyāya* considers two kinds of testimonies as valid, namely, Vedic and secular. The Vedic testimony is considered perfect and infallible due to the Veda's position as authoritative and being transferred to human world through higher beings or Gods. On the other hand, secular testimony is fallible for it is provided by human beings who are liable to erroneous understanding.[15]

4.4.2 *Prameya*

As discussed in the previous section, the *Nyāya Sūtra* mentions sixteen entities to arrive at correct knowledge. While *Pramāṇa* being the first entity means the modes of attaining knowledge, *Prameya* is the object of knowledge or the object that is known. Nyāya Sūtra tells us that there are twelve objects that can be known. They are —

(i) **ātman** (the self)
(ii) the body (organic activities)
(iii) senses (smell, taste, sight)
(iv) their objects, i.e., the sensible qualities of smell, taste, color, touch and sound
(v) cognition (*buddhi*)
(vi) mind (*manas*)
(vii) activities (*Pravṛtti),* includes both good or bad
(viii) mental defects (*dośa*)
(ix) rebirth after death and result of our good or bad actions
(x) the experiences of pleasure and pain
(xi) suffering (*dukkha*)
(xii) liberation or freedom from suffering (*apavarga*), the cessation of all suffering forever.

---

[14] *Ibid*, p.180
[15] *Ibid*, p.180

4.4.3 *Samśaya* or Doubt

The term *samśaya* means doubt. In the context of the subject matter of *nyāya,* which deals primarily with the notion of arriving at correct knowledge, 'doubt' forms an integral feature. Doubt is a stage or state of uncertainty which quite notably, forms the preceding stage in the process of *nyāya. Samśaya,* as the *Nyāya* theory explains, is a stage when the mind wavers between two contrary description of the same object and both the descriptions have the possibility of being true

4.4.4 *Prayojana* or Purpose

Prayojana clearly relates to the term purpose or the objective of a desired act. The goal which one aims to reach determines a purpose and leads to the application of principles of *nyāya.*

4.4.5 *Dṛṣtānta* or Example (Required in Inference)

Dṛṣtānta means example or an instance which represents an undisputed fact that illustrates a rule. An ordinary person and a critical thinker or a philosopher may agree and relate or agree to a *dṛṣtānta. Dṛṣtānta* or example forms an important component of reasoning and comprehending valid knowledge. For instance, one may argue that the hill must be fiery because it is smoky. The relation of fire and smoke is evoked and in such a context the kitchen may be cited as a *dṛṣtānta* example of smoke accompanying fire.

4.4.6 *Siddhānta* or Conclusion

Siddhānta may be translated as a conclusive view. *Siddhānta* is the definite ascertainment of an entity. *Siddhānta* belongs to the domain of *śāstra* or a discipline or science. Gautama's *Nyāya Sūtra* divides it into four kinds:

(i) *sarvatantra siddhānta*: a conclusion which is undisputed by any of science or discipline.

(ii) *pratitantra siddhānta*: a conclusion established by a specific discipline or by particular philosophers.

(iii) *adhikaraṇa siddhānta*: a conclusion derived by establishing the property of a given thing only after establishing another property of it.

(iv) *abhyupagama siddhānta*: a conclusion accepted provisionally by the other.

4.4.7 *Avayava* or Components of an Inference

Avayava is 'member' or 'premises.' For instance, a syllogism comprises of five premises which may be discussed below:

- there is fire on the hill (the first stage is an assertion which is the proposition to be proved).

- because there is smoke (the second stage states the reason).
- wherever there is smoke, there is fire (the third stage is illustrative in which something follows the other).
- as in the case of the kitchen (the fourth stage forms an example).
- there is fire on the hill (it is a conclusive statement).

4.4.8 *Tarka* or Counterfactual Argument

Tarka in the *Nyāya Sūtra* means a counterfactual argument and is used as an indirect way to justify a conclusion. In *tarka,* there may be a hypothetical argument. *Tarka* usually functions to eliminate absurd conclusions or consequences. A hypothetical argument of such a nature is designed to strengthen inferential cognition and also remove the possibility of doubt.

4.4.9 *Nirṇaya*

The ultimate ascertainment of true knowledge is *nirṇaya*. It is attained through pramāṇas and by elimination of all preceding and possible doubts.

4.4.10 *Vāda*

Vāda is an analytic consideration to ascertain the true knowledge. It proceeds by way of *pramāṇa* and *tarka.* The aim of vāda is not to refute an established knowledge or theory but to arrive at the truth. In *vāda,* the proponent as well as the opponent attempts to establish his own position and refute the position of the other.

4.4.11 *Jalpa*

Jalpa is brawling or haggling in which the disputing parties attempt to defeat each other, rather than establishing or ascertaining the truth. In *jalpa,* there is the use of invalid reasoning and argumentation since the primary goal is to defeat the other side.

4.4.12 *Vitaṇḍā*

Vitaṇḍā is the aim of one of the disputing sides to refute the position of the opponent rather than establishing his own side of argument. While *jalpa* aims to gain victory even by invalid argument, *vitaṇḍā* aims to win by refuting.

4.4.13 *Hetvābhāsas*

According to Gautama hetvābhāsas is a fallacious fact or evidence, because they do not have all the characteristics of true evidence. Providing a peudo *hetu* is *hetvābhāsas. Hetvābhāsas* prevents an inference from taking place.

4.4.14 *Chala*

In *chala* one of the disputing parties after failing to give a effective argument against the opponent rather gives irrelevant or pretentious responses. Unfair replies are sought in order to contradict the other side.

4.4.15 *Jāti*

Jāti means those fruitless and ineffectual arguments given by either a proponent or an opponent against the other side. Such arguments instead of destroying the opponent's position goes contrary to the position of the one who advances those arguments.

4.4.16 *Nigrahasthāna*

The last entity of Gautama's list is *nigrahasthāna.* The term *nigraha* means defeat and *sthāna* means place . It means the ultimate defeat of the proponent or the opponent and includes various types of arguments leading to the final defeat of either the proponent or the opponent. The *Nyāya Sūtra*s also enlists about twenty two types of arguments that lead to final defeat.

Ancient India had a rich tradition of argumentation. It is evident from the diverse array of literature of various schools of philosophies which have come down to us. *Nyāya* was among the foremost Schools of thought. Attempting to search for true knowledge and differentiating truth from false knowledge through rational discourse was the primary aim of all the Schools. The philosophy and methods of *Nyāya* School was applied in various domains, one of the most primary being the field of law and jurisprudence which will become evident as we proceed to the next section.

4.5 NYĀYA AS JURISPRUDENCE

So far we have discussed *Nyāya* as a school of thought and a philosophy with diverse concepts characterizing it. Let us now proceed towards the application of *nyāya* in various domains. The primary domain of application of *nyāya* method included ancient Indian law codes or the *dharmaśāstra* tradition and by implication included the political and juridical administration. One of the most profound concepts in *nyāya* is the notion of *pramāṇa* which is the means by which one obtains accurate and valid knowledge. *Dharmaśāstra* refers to a series of textual corpus dealing with jurisprudence with one of the essential components of the texts being legal administration and settlement of disputes. It is in this context that the concept of *pramāṇa* as a method of validating the truth was applied to its greatest extent. In this context, the remark of Vatsyāyana is pertinent. He remarks, "*nyāya* functions neither with regard to things unknown nor with regard to things definitely known, but it functions with only regard to things doubtful." The Indian teacher of the techniques of dispute settlement would indeed be a specialist in a branch of the *sastra* , but unless he projected his study as a facet of the attainment of truth, as any other science does, he would not be a *dharmasastri*.

"Justice," "rules," "method," or "judgment" in literal translation, is Nyaya, one of the six astika schools of Indian philosophy. The methodical development of the logic theory was this school's most significant contribution to Indian philosophy.Four of the six Pramanas—Pratyaksha (perception), Anumana (inference), Upamana (comparison and analogy), and Shabda (word)—are acknowledged by Nyaya schools as reliable sources of knowledge.

In terms of metaphysics, there are more similarities than differences between the Vaisheshika school of Hinduism and the Nyaya school. Based on this hypothesis, mistakes made when acting without sufficient knowledge lead to human misery.

In accordance with this, accurate understanding leads to moksha. This idea inspired Nyaya to concentrate on epistemology, a reliable means of learning the truth and avoiding false beliefs.

Theoretically, philosophy is a form of direct realism, according to Naiy Yayika academics, since humans can know all that truly exists. According to them, Anuvyavasaya is necessary for precise comprehension and thoughtful cognition.

The Nyaya Sutras, a notable collection of writings on reason and logic that are attributed to Aksapada Gautama. Their composition dates are thought to have been between the second and the sixth century BCE.

The Nyaya reasoning is attributed to the sage Gautama. Besides, his other names are Gautama, Aksapada, and Dirghatapar, referring to his inclination towards long-term penance and meditation, respectively.

4.6 MEANING AND DEFINITION OF *NITI*

It must be noted that the Sanskrit terms for rigid policy and material accumulation, "Niti" in Shukranitisara and "Artha" in Arthashastra, respectively, are used. Shukracharya says the king and his minister should follow the principles of the science of polity. Considered to be Shukracharya's moral code, niti is a part of the Dharmashastra.

The Nyaya reasoning is said to have been founded by the sage Gautama. He also goes by the names Dirghatapar, Aksapada, and Gautama, which refer to his preference for extended periods of penance and meditation, respectively.

Commonly known as *Usanas,* it is a science treatise that dates back to the Vedic period. Though some have even claimed that it is a 19th-century fabrication, modern historians maintain that the composition is from the Gupta period, or the fourth century A.D. The phrase's root is the Sanskrit word "Niti," which translates to "head providing proper guidance" in English.

The general well-being of the people and the State depends on the morals that Shukra Niti stresses. Shukracharya claims that although one can live without grammar, logic, or Vedanta, one cannot live without Niti, characterizing it as an essential element required to maintain social order in society.

A realization centered perspective's basic concept is that justice cannot be divorced from the true reality that emerges. While rules and institutions undoubtedly shape reality and are an essential part of it, reality as it is perceived transcends organizational bounds. This disparity has been proven to be highly significant in the history of theories of justice, especially those from Europe and the West. The two different Sanskrit terms for justice, Nyaya and Niti, actually help us discern between these two different concentrations. Of course, terms such as "niti" and "nyaya" were used in many different ways in different philosophical and legal contexts in ancient India, but the concentrations of the two concepts are fundamentally different.

4.7 SHUKRA *NITI*

Shukra Niti, also called Shukraniti, is considered to be Shukracharya's moral code and is included in Dharmashastra. The science of governance is explained in this text, with a focus on using political science ideas to raise moral standards.

Reportedly originating in the Vedic era, Shukracharya, also called *Usanas*, is credited with creating the code. However, some contemporary historians contend that the composition is a forgery, dating it to the fourth century AD, during the Gupta dynasty.

The term Niti originates from the Sanskrit verb "To head," which signifies proper guiding. Shukraniti places a strong emphasis on morality, which it contends is necessary for both the state and the population's overall well-being. As a result, attempts are made to regulate the social, political, and economic dimensions of human conduct.

According to Shukraniti, these actions are not permissible in the absence of a regulation, and the king's main responsibility should be to defend the wrongdoers. Shuracharya describes Niti as an essential element required to maintain social order in society, stating that although a person can function without grammar, reasoning, or Vedanta, they cannot function without it.

4.8 *SMRITIS*: THE *PURANAS*

The *Puranas* provide much that modern Hinduism can learn. *Puranas* are considered "very old" or "ancient" literature, with the works claiming to be older than the Vedas. Still, scholars think these texts—which talk about the so-called "later deities" Brahma, Vishnu, and Shiva—are more contemporary.

Although there are more books, the eighteen main *Puranas* are regarded as maha (great). Each of these three sets of six books corresponds to a trimurty. Some Hindus say that each pair is suitable for readers who find inspiration in the corresponding gunas.

There are also eighteen *upa puranas*. Numerous subjects are covered in the *Puranas*, such as creation, the patriarchy and gods' genealogy, morality, depictions of the world, and a number of well-known myths and stories. Some of them are repeated aloud frequently in public, such as the Vishnu Bhagvata and Daibhagavata *Puranas*.

4.9 THE CONCEPT OF JUSTICE

One may reasonably assume that justice is defined as granting everyone their due share or as a just, morally-responsible, and equitable deed or arrangement. In addition to being a matter of right or wrong, justice denotes a stance that someone may claim as their moral entitlement against us. The word alludes to justice in Indian ethics and jurisprudence.

Niti is characterized by acceptable behavior, institutional fairness, and sensible restrictions. Nyaya is a justice accomplished person. Dharma is a moral duty with interpretations based on reason, natural law, history, religion, and logic.

TABLE: 4.1 Different Thinker Perspective

Plato: Essential virtues—courage, justice, temperance, and knowledge.
Aristotle: Justice—proportionality, equality, and the preservation of equilibrium.
Rawls: Fairness is justice.
Nozick: Justice as the first and justifiable right.
Amartya Sen: Enabling individuals to lead fulfilling, dignified lives.
In Summary: The foundation of equality, liberty, and rights is justice.

4.9.1 Justice: Definitions

The idea of justice is complex and has numerous elements. John Locke argued that justice arises from natural law, while Aristotle and Plato supported the divine conception of justice.

- Justice, in Plato's view, is when every individual and social class fulfills their obligations to the best of their capacities and there is harmony within the soul.

Aristotle described justice as "fairness" in the allocation of resources, money, political posts, honors, prizes, fines, and other things based on the equality principle, which is arithmetical and proportionate equality. Fair distribution of resources, honors, rewards, and political posts constitutes justice, according to John Rawls. Robert Nozick's entitlement theory of justice maintains that the allocation of holdings (properties) within a community is just and that each person in that society has a claim to their original circumstances. Prof. Amartya Sen defines justice as: maximizing people's freedom and capacity everywhere and reducing flagrant injustice through the mobilization of resources from multiple sources and practical reasoning. J.S. Mill asserts that justice is perfect responsibility.

4.9.2 Types of Justice

Procedural Justice

Justice based on rules or procedures that are reasonable, fair, and transparent equitable allocation of benefits, duties, and commodities and services; when equality of status, respect for one's own dignity, and the fulfillment of fundamental human needs are guaranteed by the state, society, or the community, distributive justice may also be a sign of social justice.

Retributive Justice

Global justice refers to seeking justice on a worldwide scale; restorative justice focuses on helping the offender make apologies for harm done to the victim and assisting in their return to society. Justice is a fair and just penalty for wrongdoing.

4.10 NITI: INSTITUTIONAL AND ARRANGEMENT FOCUSED PERSPECTIVE ON JUSTICE

In the pursuit of justice, Niti refers to fair and just policies, practices, institutional arrangements, organizational etiquette, and proper behavior. An absolutely just society is its aim. It searches for the best possible combination of governing principles and institutional structure to guarantee that justice is done everywhere. It needs a particular kind of sociocultural environment and civilization. For instance: The Rawlsian theory of justice is predicated on the premise that fundamental values such as fairness are widely shared in a liberal society.

It comes from ideas of the social contract, which maintain that an imagined compact between the members of a community determines the social arrangements based on certain reasonable and equitable principles. To guarantee the application of the established policies, procedures, and institutional frameworks, a sovereign state is needed. For this reason, Niti is a type of procedural justice. Fair outcomes can be achieved by establishing fair standards and procedures and ensuring that institutional mechanisms are in place to enforce them. Niti brings up ideas like fair play, resource distribution, and basic societal ideals, among other things. Four principles underpin procedural justice: impartiality in decision-making, fairness in processes, transparency in behavior, and allowing people a voice. Generally in line with liberalist individualistic philosophy, which emphasizes the need for strong institutional frameworks to guarantee that self-interested, logical people act in the proper manner. Thus, Niti is formal, procedural, legal, and institutional justice. Here are a few examples: Theory of justice by John Rawls (theory of justice, 1971), Robert Nozick (Anarchy, State of Utopia, 1974), Ronald Dworkin (Sovereign Virtue, 2000), and David Gauthier (justice as Mutual advantage).

4.11 NYAYA: REALIZATION FOCUSED PERSPECTIVE ON JUSTICE

According to Prof. Sen, nyaya denotes the real achievement of justice or the abolition of extreme injustice in numerous groups and sociocultural contexts. Matasya Nyaya was a symbol of naked injustice. Rather than searching for a universal framework or ideal, Nyaya is action-oriented and acknowledges a range of values and principles in order to accomplish justice. Instead of aiming for totally egalitarian communities, Nyaya works to improve social justice by gradually eradicating the most egregious instances of inequality. It does away with the need to prioritize injustices and universal consensus (perfect rank ordering).

For establishing justice world government or globally sovereign government is not necessary. By utilizing various institutional frameworks, values, and situations, the Nyaya approach has the potential to eliminate extreme injustice in various global cultures.

Anywhere in the world, it might improve human agency's capacities and freedom. Additionally, it might contribute to a less unfair and inequitable world. As a result, Nyaya takes an action-oriented, pragmatic, deliberative, multicultural, and pluralistic approach to achieving justice.

It identifies and eradicates egregious injustice worldwide using the methods of social choice theory and public practical reasoning (partial rank ordering). It focuses on real-world societies, their socio-cultural contexts, people's actual behaviors, values, and ways to make the world more or less unjust, unfair, and unequitable rather than on just and fair institutions, rules, or principles.

In contrast to Niti, Nyaya is not constrained by national borders and does not need a sovereign state. Global justice could result from a Nyaya perspective. Since it expands to include open impartiality in place of closed impartiality and injustice.

4.12 NYAYA AND NITI ACCORDING TO THE THINKERS OF ANCIENT INDIA

Numerous techniques were used in the Niti and judicial systems of ancient India to control everyone's behavior. For instance, in the area of criminal law, suitable criteria for punishment were provided, and the severity of the charges established the proper degree of punishment. It is also known from the study of ancient scriptures that there was no firm belief on the "death penalty" throughout the time of ancient India. The scriptures of ancient India included provisions for penalizing both the consumer and their opposition, as well as for violating the procedure and the consumer's interest. Environmental significance was also prioritized.

The administrative and judicial systems of today would have been known to be continuing in the same direction as it used to be in Ancient India. The study of old books such as the Manusmriti and Grantha *Arthashastra,* as presented by Kautilya and Kaudilya, also imparts knowledge and explains how the government once carried out its duties through its departments and in some way provided Nyaya and Niti.

4.13 KAUTILYA'S VIEW ON NYAYA AND NITI

Kautilya also placed a strong focus on everyone adhering to their own religion, according to scholars from antiquity. According to his belief, adhering to *swadharma* not only results in the creation of the current system, but it also enhances the hereafter. The typical citizen nevertheless breaks the law in a variety of ways. In order to punish them, Kautilya also sets up legal procedures.

Because, in his view, the people are bereft of religion, purpose, employment, and salvation without Nyaya, and because the subjects' ultimate objective can only be achieved through Nyaya, Kautilya has placed a great deal of importance on Nyaya and Niti. Nyaya is the state's lifeblood, in his opinion.

Kautilya's Judge Selection

The king received the economic foundation of Nyaya from Kautilya. He claims that there is a good, obedient, and public welfare monarch. He nevertheless appoints judges in order to fortify the legal system. He thought that a higher court should consist of an **Amrtyas** and three religious judges who could convene and make appropriate decisions on disagreements. Kautilya delegated to the king the duty of selecting these judges. Kautilya's entire judicial system is modern. He was a strong proponent of fair Nyaya and the decentralization of the legal system. He stressed that the three judges who currently make up the higher court's pillars—a multi-member judicial bench—must be selected by majority or consensus.

4.14 MANU'S VIEWS ON NYAYA AND NITI

Aside from the establishment of a council for the purpose of crafting Manu law and the Nyaya system, the people had the liberty to establish their own regulations via federal organizations. Total, caste, and category are included. She also used to accept the regulations established by these self-made institutions, taking it as permission from the monarch. A more detailed description of the legislature's makeup is provided by Manu. He believes that there should be roughly ton of members in the legislature and council, but the foundation of their makeup should be intellectual rather than numerical.

4.14.1 Manu View's the Ideas of Punishment

Manu believes that human nature is divided into two categories: heavenly and demonic. The divine tendency also encouraged labor to make other people happy and kept in mind peace, goodness, and other people's rights. Conversely, Manu claims that this inclination simply serves to stir up excitement, unrest, and chaos in society and that it also gives man a sense of progress and makes it impossible for him to follow his faith. The devil's nature, on the other hand, allows the judicial rights of others to be grabbed solely for self-interest. Manu expresses his opinions plainly and emphasizes the necessity of using punishment to change people's behavior so they can adhere to their religion.

4.15 PRINCIPLES OF NYAYA

When everyone was discussing the utilitarian idea of promoting the happiness of the majority of people or the welfare of society as a whole, John Rawls' "theory of Nyaya" became prominent. The idea of "Nyaya" was the last to be discussed. The classical usage principle was thought to have some alternatives, including the Rawls' Nyaya principle. Based on the idea that Nyaya is a system of collaboration for mutual advantages amongst individuals living inside a society, Rawls developed his distributive Nyaya theory. As such, it displays a tension between the recognition of common interests and the interests of individuals. The Nyaya principles must serve as the foundation for defining the advantages and disadvantages of social collaboration.

It is important for everyone to understand that fairness is the foundation of the Nyaya principle, which Rawls introduced through the social contract theory. It's important to distinguish between people's subjective self-discrimination and their true judgments about Nyaya, which they do have, according to Rawls. Using these kinds of measures is bound to result in discrepancies. Therefore, it's critical to adjust one's own judgment in order to arrive at equilibrium where two conditions are met.

4.15.1 First Principale of Nyaya

Rawls begins with a moral assumption that Nyaya is associated with fariness, based on his intricate theory. He takes this stance in order to get at what is known as the "basic condition," which is the core idea of member Nyay. According to Rawls, the "original situation" is nothing more than the imagination of people in made-up situations who are imposed with a "veil of ignorance" that prevents them from learning about their status (gender, ethnicity, economic standing, intelligence, etc.) and their conception of what constitutes a "good life as well as well-being." Nobody in Rawls' talks is certain of their position in society, their social standing, their class, or how they will be treated in terms of value, intelligence, power, shared resources, etc. Furthermore, neither party is aware of the other's opinions or personal characteristics. The only way the Nyaya principles are realized is through the veil of ignorance.This guarantees that a person's choice of principles will not be influenced by social conditions or the chance of a given opportunity.

It is possible to argue that the principles of Nyaya are solely the product of initial agreement or contract because everyone is in an equal position and no one can create principles that support their own viewpoint. When choosing the "basic principles of Nyaya," Rawls designed the "basic position" as an impartial method that is to be applied in the framework of the organization's core values. This ensures legitimacy and comprehensiveness by excluding individual interests.

The contract will be upheld once the curtain of ignorance is lifted, and once individuals stray from their initial positions, it is essentially a kind of radical equalitarian liberalism with the necessary consideration given to the idea that one person shouldn't pursue their own interests to the exclusion of others.

4.15.2 Second Principle of Nyaya

Generally, the goal can be attained by applying John Rawls' fundamental Nyaya concepts. When it comes to wealth distribution, there is no sure way to know the answer because, in the ignorance of the moment, everyone would prefer to act honorably once they are above the surface of ignorance. All the fundamental liberties that a member of the minority community has demanded will also be taken away by him, including freedom of conscience, religion, and the right to life. It is the majority that is committing atrocities on minorities.

As a defense of the just principles of political freedom, Rawls incorporated this (political liberalism) idea into his book. Because "equally talented and motivated citizens have a common chance to influence government Niti and gain authority positions, even if not by social and economic class," political freedom must be valued fairly.

Rawls argues that social and economic inequality ought to be designed to favor the least inconvenienced party. People who are ignorant are unaware of the system they will be assigned to. When the curtain falls, they will either be wealthy or impoverished, well or ill. In order to make sure that everyone is protected, it is therefore advisable to set up a system wherein income is distributed fairly and only those economic and social disparities that serve the least number of people will be permitted.

In a hypothetical scenario of primordial equality, where people's vested interests are unknown to them, John Rawls assumed that a unique set of "two principles of justice" would be unanimously chosen. This assumes that there is essentially only one type of impartial argument—aside from vested interests—that satisfies the requirements of fairness. Without providing strong justifications to rule out any other options that could rival John Rawls' extremely unique formula for unbiased attention, John Rawls identifies one of these formulas among several that are accessible.

Rawls acknowledges that different citizens will naturally have different opinions about what constitutes the most reasonable kind of political justice. According to Rawls, a person ought to have equal access to opportunities in the form of their inherent potential. A person should be able to apply for "office and position" regardless of their gender, race, or social background if there is proper equality of opportunity.

4.16 NITI SARA OF KANADAKI

Niti sara, also known as Nitisara of Kanandaki, is an old Indian treatise on politics and statecraft. Kamandaka, also known as Kanandaki or Kamandakiya, was a student of Chanakya and gave his approval. In actuality, it is a recension based on the fourth-century BCE Sukara Nitisara. Conventionally, it is dated to the fourth or third century BCE, although more recent research positions it broadly between the Gupta and Harsha periods, in the third and seventh centuries CE. In total, there are nineteen sections. The work is dedicated to Patliputra's Chandragupta. Academics assume that the work was modeled after the Hitopadesha. Nitisara consists of thirty-sargas (chapters) and thirty-six prakaranas.

Based on the Kautilya Arthasastra, it addresses a wide range of social issues, such as theories of social order, state structure, ruler responsibilities, governmental organization, relationships between principles, the ethics of envoys and spies, the use of different political instruments, battalion array varieties, moral altitude, and so forth. Unlike Arthasastra, which placed emphasis on carrying out royal duties, Nitisara highlights color and the emperor's military might. In Sukra's own writing, Kanandaka refers to his treaties with the little (Nitisara).

The nitisastra was made ready by Lord Brahma. In addition to keeping people utilizing things in the same manner for a very long time, nitisara is the source of all people's livelihood. Beginning with nitisastra, the source of riches, desire, and virtue is claimed to exist in the book. In addition to bestowing blessings, kings ought to study it thoroughly and apply its knowledge to subjugate other realms. Should the king give up Niti and become self-willed (svatantra), he will suffer. It is thus the sine qua non of the king's well-functioning government, nitisastra.

It does, however, invariably accomplish a higher goal as well because it serves far more objectives than just the king's interests. From Nitisastra all animals receive their nourishment, and customs toward men are maintained. Before addressing the following problem, the author presents an argument that contradicts the findings of prior studies. In contrast to the King's inculcation of discipline, the author used punishment, or "danda," as an example of statecraft. The monarch is emphasized the importance of self-discipline and intellectual training early in the text by Ramasdaka, who is just extending Kautilya's rules in this area.

4.17 COMPARATIVE NYAYA

Sen argues that Rawls' idea of "transcendental Institutionalism" is essentially a moral presumption, one that he develops but is ultimately moulded by certain limitations. Sen argues that the biggest flaw in Rawls' theory of Nyaya presentation is transcendental institutionalism.

Drawing on the tradition of social interaction, Rawls' theory aims to elucidate certain notions that are critical to the establishment of public institutions required for a just society. He emphasized that rather than focusing on the characteristics of just societies, many of the Nyaya principles should include ways to minimize and increase Nyaya. Sen consequently considered the main problem with Rawls' theory to be the perfection doctrine's disconnection from reality.

Prof. Sen's view of Nyaya as a genuine tactic makes it easier to understand why it is so important to prevent Nyaya from getting known to the public. He describes it as the exact reverse of Rawls' argument about a just or utopian society. Nyaya is "Nyaya" equal to justice, in Rawls' opinion. However, what justification does Rawls find for Nyaya? In what situations could Nyaya be considered "Fairness"?

Regarding it, Rawls provides us with two of the Nyaya Fundamental Principles. When Rawls established the concept of Nyaya, it was influenced by Kantian theological ethics. A broad form of ethics that is primarily founded on moral precepts is Kantian deontological ethics.

As stated by Chris Brown, Sen challenges us to use public reasoning to pursue justice throughout "The Idea of Justice". We are to compare the effects of different policies and consider the methods used in the name of impartiality and fairness, rather than referring to some ideal.

He asks us to embrace nyaya rather than niti, Smith rather than Kant, and to view social systems as wholes, evaluating their effects in general terms without getting fixated on formalities or processes. Public reasoning of this nature can no longer be limited to certain societies; rather, it must now have a global reach.

Luckily, our interconnectedness, which compels us to consider others' interests, also makes it easier for us to understand their viewpoint. Sen knows it's going to be difficult. The comparisons he asks us to draw will make us question our own interests, which is never easy, and there is no ideal to steer our debates toward. He nevertheless provides us with a model of what it means to be a worldwide, objective observer through his own work and, in fact, through his own life.[16]

Economist Amartya Sen published a book in 2009 called "The Idea of Justice". The piece is a reworking and analysis of John Rawls' "A Theory of Justice (1971)". The book's primary goal is to revise and evaluate the foundational ideas put forward by John Rawls in "A Theory of Justice (1971)". Sen drew extensively on Rawls' publications, most of which were composed during the latter's tenure as an Indian professor. Sen's approach centered on developing a theory that would empower common people to take actions in the direction of a more just society. These are the main issues that Amartya Sen addresses in this book: Sen argues that addressing injustice is just as important to people as advancing their own interests. This sentence carries an obvious consequence. Because people are naturally motivated to eliminate injustice wherever it arises, institutions don't really matter that much. To prevent transgressions and to foster a feeling of fairness in people, ideal organizations do not need to impose strict restrictions on specific individuals.[17]

Sen describes 'plural grounding' as a 'overlapping consensus' (to use Rawls' terminology) between individuals of different ideologies, belief systems, or value systems that enables people to agree on comparative assessments of justice without having to agree on all of their values and beliefs. 'Public Reason,' that is, free discourse and reasoned argument, can facilitate this. This is a result of people's innate desire to end injustice that can be fixed.

---

[16] Brown, Chris, On Amartya Sen and The idea of justice, Ethics and International Affairs, 24 (3). pp. 309–318, 2010.

[17] Amartya Sen, "Introduction" in The Idea of Justice, Harvard University Press, 2009.

Sen argues, among other things, that social fairness is a goal that cannot be classified as either accomplished or not. Rather, he argues that justice should be evaluated as a spectrum and should be understood as such. Furthermore, he argues that evaluating the equity of different groups can be done without needing an already formed abstract ideal of justice. He contends that it is feasible to meaningfully assess the level of justice in two groups without advancing an ideal, transcendent view of justice. The other side, he says, is transcendental institutionalism.[18]

Sen defends justice as fairness, which is one of Rawls' central theoretical tenets. Although he disapproves of the necessity of Rawls' two principles of justice, which resulted from the initial position thought experiment in "A Theory of Justice", he nevertheless considers this nebulous concept—which is challenging to implement in any given situation—to be among Rawls' best concepts.[19] Sen's thesis that The Theory of Moral Sentiments (1759), the first major book of Adam Smith, is both the most important and unduly overlooked of Smith's writings draws heavily on this work.

"The theory of justice must be more concerned with the elimination of removable injustices rather than defining a perfectly just society," Prof. Amartya Sen stated. Talking about his latest book, which is titled "Demand for Justice in India," Sen suggested turning back to the classical Hindu philosophy that examines the concepts of Niti and Nyaya in order to approach the difficult subject of justice and its relevance in everyday life.

In Sanskrit legal philosophy, just laws and institutions are referred to as niti, while their actualization is referred to as nyaya. If niti were fully implemented, it would be an abstract activity that maximizes justice and public good. Nyaya, on the other hand, is about abiding by the laws and regulations.[20] Sen spoke about affirmative action in India, saying that although Niti is the driving force behind the program, Nyaya should serve as its foundation. He made the argument that affirmative action had its limitations.[21].

Consider the two separate terminology, niti and nyaya, that are utilized in a customary legal distinction in India. In traditional Sanskrit, both words refer to justice. The phrases "niti" are generally used in relation to organizational propriety and behavioral correctness. In contrast to niti, nyaya denotes a deeper comprehension of successfully carried out justice. That school of thought holds that all factors, including institutions, rules, and organizational roles, regardless of their importance, must be analyzed

---

[18] Amartya Sen, "Introduction" in The Idea of Justice, Harvard University Press, 2009.

[19] *Ibid.*

[20] Neha Sakhuja, *Asia Society Northern California*, AsiaSociety.org 2004 interview with Amartya Sen.

[21] *Ibid.*

from the larger, more inclusive perspective of nyaya, which is inextricably linked to the reality that actually emerges and not just the rules and institutions we happen to have.[22]

Amartya Sen draws attention to the idea of justice by framing The Idea of Justice as a reason to examine how society is acting unjustly. It talks about ways to make society more equitable and how important it is to acknowledge that the pursuit of justice is an ongoing process. Arguments against social problems are covered in this book together with inspirational statements about what is morally and vital for society. The principles outlined in the country's Constitution are embodied in the Idea of Justice, a guiding principle that all citizens of the nation are required to see, strive for, and protect.

This concept, with its qualities of honesty, generosity, equality, tolerance, power, and integrity, is like a torch that spreads the light of a country's beliefs. Sen thus contends that advancing one's own interests is not more important to people than eliminating injustice. This assertion carries a clear consequence. Institutions don't really matter because people are naturally motivated to eradicate injustice wherever it arises.[23]

Since Rawls' interpretation of Nyaya is tenable, it is not advisable to debate whether it is better than Sen's. Sen addresses nyaya with a niti approach and insists on rejecting orthodoxy since the state is seen as an institution, making his approach to nyaya both exclusionary and institutionalist.

The central thesis of Nyaya is that national laws are too narrow a prism through which to view, evaluate, and challenge the global nature of our world. These are the local, home perspectives on Nyaya that are taken into account in two different ways. Secondly, ignoring the global context in favor of national law ignores one of the main challenges in the fight against Nyaya. Sen calls for a greater focus on global, comparative, and most importantly, significant concerns in legal education.

Regarding the idea of the impartial audience that keeps coming up, this could result in a (perhaps significant) restructure of western legal education on a global scale. It is possible to claim that the pursuit of absolute Nyaya aims for unfathomable perfection, but the problem is that many likely nyaya scenarios are far more complicated. Sen's writings demand the elimination of major Nyaya and critique the motion of absolute Nyaya. An ideal society, according to Karl Marx, would not have workers as subordinate to other classes.

His thesis was rejected as impractical and unworkable, and so did not lead to the establishment of this society, but it did open the door for other

---

[22] Amartya Sen, "Introduction" in the Idea of Justice, Harvard University Press, 2009.

[23] *Ibid.*

economic reforms such as the abolition of labor and workers' compensation legislation. From the viewpoint of the entire community, Nyaya diminishes.

Sen draws an analogy between the decision of Matsya-Nyaya, or where big fish eat small fish, and ancient Hindu jurisprudence. This analogy is essentially the same as the current utilization theory, which cannot be said to be anxiety-free. However, both Rawls and Sen are on the same path and share similar views regarding the incorrectness of the concept of utilitarianism, or a system that only promotes the welfare of the majority or the happiness of the greatest number.

MODEL QUESTIONS FOR PRACTICE

4.1 Briefly explain the concept of Nyaya in Ancient India.

4.2 Differentiate between the concept of Nyaya and Niti.

4.3 Analyze the concept of Nyaya by John Rawls.

4.4 Analyse the concept of Nyaya or justice by Amartya Sen.

5

Sabha and Samiti

5.1 INTRODUCTION

Understanding Indian History is intrinsically linked with the study of India's remote antiquity. History as a discipline attempts to study human activities in the past and in doing so historians divide human past into several time-periods based on the major features characterizing an epoch, era, age or period. Historical periodization is broadly categorized into the following:

(i) **Prehistory:** It is that period of human history before the advent of writing systems. The term *Pre-historique* was coined by a French Geologist Paul Tournal when he discovered certain artifacts in the caves of Southern France. The word 'Prehistoric' was introduced and popularized by Daniel Wilson while referring to human evolutionary history before the invention of writing by humans. The period is alternatively known as pre-literate history. Due to the absence of written documents, historians rely primarily on archaeological material to study the period. It is important to remember that Prehistory studies all the cultural developments of human beings which include both biological evolution as well as cognitive developments. Indian Prehistory covers a long timeline and is subdivided into three broad periods—Palaeolithic Period; Mesolithic Period; and Neolithic Period. The Prehistoric period is characterized by the use of stone tools. Humans led a nomadic way of life with hunting and gathering being the primary modes of subsistence.

(ii) **Protohistory:** The term *'la Protohistorique'* was also coined by the French to refer to the transition between prehistoric to the historic period. It is the intervening period between prehistory to written or recorded history. Not every civilization or culture may begin writing at the same time. Some societies may begin writing earlier than that of their contemporaries. It has often been observed that a literate society may refer to a non-literate society in their documents. Therefore, we do find references to civilizations which may not have produced their own documents but their existence is documented by other civilizations.

(iii) **Recorded History:** Often referred to as *History* or Recorded History is the period when societies have started writing and documenting important or historical events. Writing and documentation through various medium is a conscious effort.

India is a unique example of an overlap of Protohistoric and Historic period. The historical period in India is widely held to have begun from the middle of the 1st millennium BCE with the issue of edicts (inscriptions) written in various scripts and languages by Asoka of the Mauryan empire. However, it is also important to note that writing was known, although undeciphered, in the Harappan period (3300 BCE–1300 BCE) which is much earlier than Asoka. At the same time, it is also necessary to note that the post-Harappan period, which marks the beginning of the Vedic Age was predominantly an oral culture wherein the literary accounts that were created were not documented in written form but was passed orally on from one generation to the next.

5.2 UNDERSTANDING THE VEDIC AGE

This chapter is primarily focused on two Vedic institutions—the *Sabhā* and *Samiti*. It is, therefore, important to have a basic understanding of the Vedic Age. As mentioned earlier, the Vedic period (c. 1500–c. 500 BCE) was an oral culture and does not provide us written documentation but however, is intrinsically linked with a corpus of voluminous unwritten literature. The Vedic age is momentous due to the fact that India enters its first literary phase which is highly intense, rich, prolific and erudite. Veda is a collective term for the corpus of sacred literature composed Sanskrit which is one of the oldest languages of the world. The Vedas are four in number, which are: *Rigveda, Samaveda, Yajurveda and Atharvaveda*. Scholars divide the Vedic period into two periods—Early Vedic or *Rigvedic* period and Later Vedic period—according to the chronology of their compositions. While the term *Veda* is etymologically derived from the root *vid* which means 'to know', 'knowledge' or 'wisdom', it primarily comprises of religious hymns or *mantras* dedicated to various deities and for Vedic *yajña* (fire sacrifice). These Vedic hymns despite being religious also give us significant information about the political, social and economic perspectives about the Vedic period.

The Early Vedic society had a tribal political structure and was a cattle rearing or pastoral society where cattle was the primary source of subsistence rather than agriculture. Therefore, cattle acquisition was a major component of such societies and also the most important reason for battles between tribes. We have frequent references to inter-tribal conflicts, one of the most well known being the *dasarajanya* battle or the Battle of Ten Kings mentioned in the *Rigveda*. Some of the famous names of tribes include the *Bharatas, Purus, Yadus, Druhyus,* and *Turvasus*. Cattle raids and thefts are commonly mentioned in the *Rigveda*. The term *gavishthi* (desire for cows) is used as a synonym for war is suggestive of the cattle-based society. The Early Vedic society was clan based and the *varna* or caste structure was not rigid. The *Rigvedic raja* is usually translated as king who is usually considered owner of landed property having a subject population. The *raja* on the contrary was a chief or leader and protector of the tribe and cattle. There are various epithets used for the *raja,* like *gopati* (protector of cow) or *vispati* (protector of tribe). As we proceed to the Later Vedic period, the Sanskrit speaking Vedic people most likely started settling down and apart from cattle, land also started becoming significant as property. The Later Vedic raja is now called *bhupati* (protector/lord of land).

A sabhā in Ancient India was an assembly, congregation, or council. Personified as a deity, Sabhā is a daughter of Prajapati in the *Atharvaveda*. In Epic Sanskrit, the term refers also to an assembly hall or council-chamber, and to a hostel, eating-house, or gambling-house. While the term *Jansabha* refers to large public gathering.

The Mahabharata, Book 2, has a Sabha Parva or Sabha episode, which describes the sabha under King Yudhishthira. Monier-Williams compares the word to Old English sibb "clan" (Old High German *sippa*), in Modern English surviving in the term gossip (from god-sib).

In ancient India, a sabhā was a council, assembly, or congregation. In the *Atharvaveda*, Sabhā is personified as a goddess and the daughter of *Prajapati*. The phrase in Epic Sanskrit also denotes a hostel, dining establishment, gambling house, and assembly hall or council chamber. However, a *Jansabha* is a sizable public assembly. The sabha under King *Yudhishthira* is described in the *Sabha Parva,* often known as the Sabha incident, found in Book 2 of the Mahabharata. In south India, especially in Tamil Nadu, a sabhā is a body or organization that is popularly active in promoting fine arts, including drama. Modern terminology used to refer to the Indian Parliament, such as Lok Sabha (Lower House) and Rajya Sabha (Upper House), as well as the Vidhan Sabha (Legislative Assembly) of the Indian states, have also been derived from the term Sabha. The Pratinidhi Sabha House of Representatives (Lower House), Rastriya Sabha National

Assembly (Upper House), and Pradesh Sabha (Provincial Assemblies) are referred to as the "Sabha" in the Federal Parliament of Nepal.

Both assembly and assembly hall are referred to by the name "Sabha" in early and later Rigvedic languages. In ancient India, the Sabha and the Samiti were two of the most well-liked assemblies. Their importance in Vedic state affairs was, in fact, remarkable. The Sabha is a place of dance, music, witchcraft, and sorcery; the Rigveda describes it as a place of dicing and gambling. There are nine instances of the term "Samiti" in the Rigveda and thirteen in the *Atharvaveda.* According to the Rigveda, a person could not reign without a Samiti. A vedic allusion spoke of the presence of an Rajan (ruler) in a Samiti. In another connection, a group of monarchs was seated together in a Samiti. According to the Rigveda, there were Samiti people talking about their animals. A *Rigvedic* prayer demanded that the samiti have order and coherence of mind. The Brahman priest's prayer on behalf of a Samiti was contained in the *Atharvaveda.*

The physical characteristics of the Sabha were described by the *Sabha-sthanu* (assembly-hall pillar). Several more titles related to the Sabha indicated possible participants and events that happened in the *sabha: sabha-chara, sabhasad, and sabhyas* (members of the assembly); *sabha-vati* (women members of the assembly*); sabha-pala (*guardian of the assembly*); sabha-pati (*lord of the assembly)*; sabheya and sabha-yogya (*worthy of the assembly); *and sabha-saha* (eminent in the assembly). The Rigveda states that members of the sabha prayed to the *God Indra* for protection over the assembly and its members as well as for the sabha to hear their arguments and give them weight.

None of the Vedas clearly explained the relationships between sabha, samiti, and rajans, despite the vedas' sporadic mentions of sabha, samiti, and rajans. However, this did not stop later researchers from proposing that sabhas and samitis held elections and ousted kings, collected taxes, waged war, and participated in democratic (may be even unanimous) decision-making.

It also didn't stop later researchers from drawing comparisons between the samitis and vedic sabhas, anthropological accounts of clan and tribe assemblies, Homeric agoras, Roman senates, Teuton chief councils, and Anglo-Saxon witenagemot culture. All of these experts' recommendations have to be regarded as hypothetical due to the limited number of references in the Vedas. This assembly was also attended by women known as Sabhavati. It carried out judicial, administrative, and pastoral affairs duties as well as exercising judicial authority.[1]

---

[1] Janki Nath Bhat, Ancient Indian Democracies civilization, Vol. 4.1 (1954), pp. 51–59, Available at://www.jstore.org/stable/41377595.

5.3 RAJAN SABHA AND SAMITI VIDHATA

From 1500 BC to 1000 BC was the Early Vedic Period, also known as the *Rigvedic* Period. During this period, the leader of a family was usually the eldest male in patriarchal societies known as a *"kula,"* a family served as the fundamental building block of political organization. A *"Kulapa"* was the title given to the family leader. Several of these families came together to form a *"grama."* The job of leading a "grama" fell to a local headman known as a *"Gramini."* Some communities came together to form a *"visu."* The *"Vishayapati"* was incharge of the *"visu"*. A group of *"visu"* formed a community. During the *Rigvedic* era, a community was referred to as a *"Jana,"* signifying the highest level of governmental hierarchy.[2]

Rajan

The *"Jana,"* or head of a community, was also referred to as the *"Rajan."* Rather than seeing the Rajan as a monarch, the people saw him as their defender. There was no true governmental organization or monarchy during this time. Because of his leadership qualities, Rajan was also known as *"Gopati Janasya"* or *"Janasya Gopa."* During this time, cattle wealth control was the primary reason for fighting conflicts rather than territorial claims. Rajan battled in these conflicts on behalf of his *"Jana."*

The "Sabha" and the "Samiti," two assemblies, assisted the *Rajan* in reaching crucial judgments. A *"Purohita"* helped the *Rajan* with daily administration as well. Since state territory was non-existent, the Rajan did not keep an army.[3]

5.4 SABHA AND SAMITI

The *Rigvedic* era used the term "Sabha" to refer to an assembly. The "Sabha" was attended by the more senior *Jana* members. Women who go by the name "Sabhavati" also attended this assembly. However, women ceased to attend the "Sabha" in the later Vedic period.[4] In addition to dice games and gambling, the "Sabha" also practiced music, dance, magic, and witchcraft. This assembly conducted judicial and administrative business, used its judicial power, and talked about pastoral matters. "Samiti" was the term used for the political debates and business conducted in the folk assembly. The "Rajan" was chosen by the "Samiti." The "Samiti" talked about intellectual topics in addition to political matters. A primary topic of this conference was prayers and religious activities. However, the

---

[2] Political Structure in the Early Vedic Period, Available at:https://unacademy.com/content/bpsc/study-material/history/political-structure-in-the-early-vedic-period/

[3] *Ibid.*

[4] *Ibid.*

significance of this assemblage did not develop until the late stages of the Early Vedic era.

Vidhata

The earliest tribal assembly was called Vidhata. Given that the word "Vidhata" appears 122 times in the Rigvedas, it appears to be the most significant assembly. This assembly was called to make decisions pertaining to the social, political, military, economic, and religious spheres.The Rigveda mentions women's involvement in the "Sabha" just once. On the other hand, women's involvement in the "Vidhata" is mentioned frequently. Women participated in the assembly's debates as well. During the *Rigvedic* period, this was the first known folk meeting. The "Vidhata" served as a gathering place for the many clans and tribes to worship their own gods.

The Members

The *"Purohit," "Gramani,"* and *"Senani,"* among other significant officials, helped the Rajan. The title of "Purohit" was the most distinguished and well-respected of all the officials. The son of the "Purohit" himself would typically acquire this role.

The Rajan considered the "Purohit" to be a spiritual teacher. In addition, he served as Rajan's principal advisor and went with him on missions. The "Purohit" also prayed to God for Rajan's protection and triumph. Two of the most well-known Purohits of the Early Vedic era were "Vasishta" and "Vishwamitra."

The "Senani" was in charge of leading the armed forces, while the "Gramani" served as the village official. When Rajan took his oath, both "Gramani" and "Senani," who played equally important roles, had to be present.

The Rajan was supported by a number of other officials, including "charioteer" *Suta*, "chief accountant" *Akshavapa*, "chief queen" Mahishi, "treasurer" *Sangrahita*, "messenger" *Kaata*, "lord of the royal household," and "forest chief" *Govikarta*. *Bhagadudha* was responsible for collecting revenue. Therefore, it is evident that the early Vedic era sowed the seeds for modern governance.

A family, or 'Kula,' constituted the fundamental unit of the governmental organization throughout the early Vedic era. A "Grama" was formed by the gathering of multiple families. A group of "Grama" combined to make *"Visu,"* and another group of *"Visu"* combined to form a *"Jana,"* the highest administrative stratum.

A *"Jana"* was led by a "Rajan," who was revered as the people's leader and defender. The Rajan received assistance in making judgments on a number of issues from two assemblies known as the "Sabha" and "Samiti." The people assembly was known as the "Samiti," while the elders of the tribe composed the "Sabha."

5.5 THE DIFFERENTIATIONS AND RELATIONSHIP BETWEEN SABHA AND SAMITI

The Sabha and the Samiti were the same thing in the beginning. They were referred to be Prajapati's daughters. These were mobile units under the leadership of chiefs who moved constantly with the forces. It appears that the only distinction between the Sabha and the Samiti was that the former carried out judicial duties while the latter did not. Later, the samiti vanished and the sabha shrank to a tiny aristocratic body. The *Samiti* is mentioned in the most recent books of the Rigveda, indicating that it gained significance only at the conclusion of the *Rigvedic* era. The purpose of a samiti, or folk assembly, was for tribe members to meet and conduct business. It was concerned with religious rituals and prayers as well as intellectual topics. It appears from the references that the Samiti elected and re-elected the Rajan.[5]

There are eight instances of the term "sabha" in the Rigveda and seventeen in the Atharvaveda. The word "sabha" once alluded to a gathering hall. Sabha also used the phrase "body of men shining together" in various contexts. The words "sabha" and "samiti," which both denote a conference, assembly, or council of people, were frequently used interchangeably.

According to the Atharvaveda, two daughters of the high Vedic god Prajāpati are recognized as Sabha and Samiti. Some scholars have deduced that sabhas may have existed before samitis since sabha always occurred before samiti when the terms appeared combined. However, no historical literature has distinguished between sabhas and samitis, their appearance order, or their relationships.[6]

In both of them, political choices were made through an assembly with a restricted membership and an institution based on more substantial membership deliberations; in other words, these two institutions attempted to restrain the authority of the state. In addition to Sabha and Samiti, other well-known organizations like *Vidatha, Parishad, Sangram,* and so forth are also mentioned. However, a detailed description of the assembly and committee is provided here because of their significance.

'Samiti' implies to assemble; that is, the public as a whole was present at the committee. The committee is also known by the titles *Sangati* and Sangram. There are numerous instances when the word "committee" is used, including one where the monarch is mentioned attending the committee. "I am the supreme one, who has come with the power to do all kinds of works and I will conquer your hearts, your works, and also

---

5 History of Ideas, Chapter: Political Institution of Vedic age, Sabha, Samiti and Vidatha, October 2019, Sahitya Bhavan Publication and Distribution Agra, U.P., India.

6 Political Structure in the early vedic period, Rajan, Sabha and Samiti, Vidatha.

the committee," declares the king himself in the second position. Therefore, it was thought that the king had to be on the committee. The principle of uniformity in state policy, committee composition, goal, and mentality is stated in both the *Rigveda* and the *Atharvaveda*. This makes it evident that the committee had a significant role. The election and re-election of the king was one of its major duties. This place also discusses non-political subjects. That's why it was imperative that everyone be present. As per the Atharvaveda, Samiti was the public assembly that possessed the closest bond with the sovereign. Its gatherings were place during times of national crisis, war, and monarch crowning, among other events.

A sabha was a gathering of people, and they were common in the early *Rigvedic* era. The entire community was a member of the sabha and could take part. Sabha was attended by women as well. Though occasionally it also performed judicial functions, Sabha made certain socially significant decisions on the welfare of the society.

Later on in the *Rigvedic* period, Samiti, which was also a council of people, gained popularity. Samiti was further limited to elites only. Ladies were expected to attend samiti. Samiti finally reduced to an aristocratic body. In India, the Early Vedic era is when Sabha and Samiti were first mentioned. These were significant groups that helped the administration and society find solutions to their challenges. Together with Gana and Parishad, these gatherings might have been crucial in the distribution of resources. The Sabha was an exclusive council made up mostly of individuals with positions of authority.

Some historians claim that Sabhas and Samitis are related and that Sabhas precede Samitis. Sabhapati, or the lord of the assembly, are members who were connected to the Sabha as described in the Vedas. In the early Vedic era, a family, or "Kula," constituted the fundamental unit of the governmental framework. To create a "Grama," several families banded together. A group of 'Grama' united to form a 'Visu,' while another group of 'Visu' united to form a 'Jana,' the highest administrative stratum. A council or assembly (*Sabheya*) of refined, sophisticated, well-mannered, and respectable people, the *Sabhayogya* is appropriate for society. Members of the assembly are called Sabha-chora, Sabhasad, and Sabyas, Sabhavati, the female member, Guardian, Sabhapala and keeper of the assembly Sabhavin.

5.6 MAIN FUNCTIONS OF SABHA AND SAMITI

It was an assembly of dignitaries and well-known individuals who used to make certain crucial decisions on enterprises and policies. The Rigveda mentions that it was a location for gaming, dice games, and dancing to music. It possessed judicial authority in criminal cases. In the past, members of the Sabha prayed to Lord *Indra* for protection over the body and its members. All the Clan and tribe members used to be a part of another significant assembly called a samiti. The Rigveda has nine instances of the Samiti, while the *Atharvaveda* has thirteen.

Function of Samiti

The monarch was once chosen by this method, and it's stated that their reign was temporary. The Samiti might remove the King at any time if they felt he was unfit to rule the people. Political activity is mostly dealt with. During the early Vedic era, both were equally significant; but, as time went on, Samiti gained greater significance and Sabha's influence decreased.

Sabha in Ancient India

In ancient India, the Sabha was a distinct entity that was a component of the village. The king and the sabha were connected in certain states. The Sabha was a rural gathering where people would get together to talk about political and social matters. It was a significant political division. Nobles were usually the ones who attended. It was regarded as the national adjudication body. The Rigveda makes reference to this phrase. Every task was completed by sabha members. Eventually, a sabha developed an aristocratic and patriarchal character. In the past, women attended sabhas as well. But in the later Vedic era, it ceased. The village chief, known as Gramini, was present at the Samiti sessions. Priests were in attendance at the sabha. But there is little information in the Vedic literature.

The *Rigvedic* era established the original clan nature of the sabha. The poor and destitute could not be members of the sabha. Those who possessed horses and chariots held power were members of Sabha. Sabha was the King's advisory body, and it relied on their judgment and guidance. Sabha is a gambling assembly, according to the Rigveda. Dance and song were also forms of entertainment with Sabha. Additionally, it was connected to sorcery and witchcraft. It covered pastoral matters as well. The sabha also discussed religious activity. It is believed that its members called upon Lord *Indra* to keep the sabha safe. They offered a sacrifice before every meeting.

The Sabha also performed administrative and political duties. Evidence exists to suggest that the sabha carried out judicial duties as well. There is a claim that the standing committee of the sabha, not the entire assembly, is responsible for carrying out the judicial tasks. The *Jataka* also mentions the judicial function of the sabha, indicating that it existed later. The royal presence in the sabha is also mentioned. There is proof that the king was present at the sabha. The King upheld his own sabha, according to the *Chandogya Upanishad*. The king regarded the advice of the sabha as ultimate. The Sabha was a permanent body made up of particular men.

5.7 NON-MONARCHICAL OR REPUBLIC FORM OF GOVERNMENT IN THE VEDIC PERIOD, INTERPRETATION BY JAGDISH P. SHARMA

The vajasaneyi samhita has at least six mentions of sabha and its derivatives—sabhya, sabhasad, sabhapati, sabhacara and sabhasthanu. The Maitrayani and Taiiriya samhitas aslo refer to the sabhya, sabha, and sabhasad. The satapatha Brahmana and the Taittiriya Brahmana refer to the sabha at least 9 times, the Kathaka Samhita, the Kausitaki Brahmana and Chandogya Upanisad also make mention of sabha, sabhapati and sabhasad.[7]

The Brahmanas versed in sacrificial lore and performedthe actual sacrific eor assisted in its performance were designated as vidathyas. According to Professor sharma, Vidatha was the earliest folk-assembly of the Indo-aryans which undertook multifarious activities, economic, military, distributive etc. on behalf of the whole tribe, cannot be substantiated. On the other side vedic literature explianed vidatha was a local congregation performing mainly religious rites and ceremonies for the good luck and prosperity of the settlement.[8]

Republican form of government under the *vajjian* confederacy during the emergency of Buddhism-Buddhist period.

- The Licchavis of Vaishali
- The Videha of Mithila
- The Neyas of Kundapura
- The Mallas of Pava and Kusinara
- The Sakya of Kapilavasthu
- The Koligyas of Ramagama

Non-Monarchial Government in Vedic India

1. Government with a Ruler chosen by the *Vis* (Head of the Family)
2. Government of the Sabha
3. Government of Sabha and the Samiti
4. Government of the Rajas and the Samiti
5. Government with a single king, sabha as his court, samiti-parishad

It was not Republicanism. It was Aristocratic, Oligarchic, or at best limited monarchies.

---

[7] Jagadish P. Sharma, "Non-Monarchical Governments in Vedic India", *Republics in Ancient India*, Brill, Leiden, 1968, p. 34.

[8] *Ibid.*

Sources

Rigveda

- 8 references of sabha;
- 9 references of samiti

Atharvaveda

- 17 references of Sabha; 13 references of samiti
- Refer Sabha and Samiti as two daughters of Prajapati

Brahmanas—Vedic Sruti works

- Aitareya Brahmana, Jaiminiya Brahmana, Satapatha Brahmana.
- Upnishadas—Vedantic Philosophy.
- Byhaddranyaka Upanisad, Chandogya Upanisad.
- Other Samhitas (hymns & mantras) of vedic period
- Vajasaneye Samhita, Kathaka samhita.

Buddhist Texts such as

- Digha Nihdya, Mahaparinarvana Sutta, and Buddhist stories Jatakas.

Jain Text

Interpretation of these texts by noted historians, and thinkers such as

- Shama Sastri, Bloomfield, Zimmer and Majumdar specifically interpretated and worked upon the Electoral Process of non-monarchical government.
- Rhys Davids, K.P. Jayaswal, R.C. Majumdar, R.S. Sharma, Zimmer, Ludurig, Altekar, T.P. Sharma.

5.8 NOMENCLATURE OF INSTITUTIONS OF ANCIENT INDIA

5.8.1 Structures of the Institutions

- **Vedic people:** Aryans, farming cattle raising and hunting community.
- **Gana, Sangha,** *Jana*: The people of political community.
- **Clan** consisting of many families; also denoted community, tribe, race, subject, people.

  A body composed of heads of families of the political community.
- **Vispati:** head of the clan.
- **Sabha:** Aristocratic oligarchy. Composed of best, richest and strongest men.
- **Samiti:** Assembly of Commoners.

- **Vidhata:** Assembly of early vedic period meant for secular, religious and military purpose.
- **Government** with a ruler chosen by the Vis—popular Monarchy.

Earliest version of political organization of the Aryans during pre-*Rigvedic* period.[9]

- **King** chosen or selected by heads of families. **Kingship** was non-heriditary, but appointed for life. King could be removed or banished and reinstated. The King was the best, richest and strongest men. King had power, vigour and heroism; he was great orator, expert in chariot racing and dice contest. King was commander of armies, but perhaps not the supreme judge. Important men of the Vis had the real authority. Territorial boundaries of such political communities kept shifting.

5.8.2 Government of the Sabha

- Sabha, as an aristocratic council, had supreme power of governance. There seems to be no king, nor samiti.
- Head of Sabha, Sabhapati, was first among equal. Such governance model was mixture of Oligarchy and Aristocracy.
- **Probable Timeline:** During Rigveda, earlier than when both sabha and samiti existed.
- **Nomenclature**

  Sabhaya, Sabheya, Sabhaga, Sabhavan: member of sabha.

  Sabhasad: Sabha member performing judicial functions. One superior or eminent member of Sabha.

  Sabhapati: President of Sabha.

  Sabha: meeting hall, council hall, court, sabhagara.

  Council hall: political meeting, governance decision, dispensation of justice, religious functions, entertainment—dice games, dancing, music, withcraft, magic, etc.
- **Role of Sabhasads, Sabhapati:** decided war and peace, administered justice, performed religious rites.
- **Qualities for Sabhya:** Strength, expert in warfare, courage, valour, oratory, learning, wealth, family men above age of 30–35 preferred.
- **Sabhavati:** Women warthy of going to Sabha.
- **Number of sabha Members:** May be in 100s or 1000s.[10]

---

9 Jagadish P. Sharma, "Non-Monarchical Governments in Vedic India", *Republics in Ancient India,* Brill, Leiden, 1968, p. 34.

10 Jagadish P. Sharma, "Non-Monarchical Governments in Vedic India", *Republics*

5.8.3 Government of the Sabha and the Samiti

- Only in Atharvaveda, Sabha and the Samiti mentioned in same verse.
- Hence, this form of government might have appeared after the government by Sabha.
- Rule by Sabha, a smaller but more powerful aristocratic council and samiti, larger assembly of all the heads of family of the political community.
- Samiti, perhaps, developed from pre-*Rigvedic*.
- Samiti together with Sabha, governed the community.
- Samiti put a check on the power of Sabha.
- Ultimate authority was probably vested in the Samiti, but in practice Sabha had the real power of governance.
- Atharvaveda called them (Sabha and Samiti) daughters of Prajapati.
- There was *No King*, denoted Republican form of government, comparatively more democratic.
- Both had powers to deliberate on matters of importance.
- Sometimes there might be joint session of Sabha and Samiti.
- It might indicate disagreement between the two bodies on some matters.
- Members of Sabha might attend the meeting of Samiti.
- Speakers in both these bodies, had to be polite and pleasant in order to win the favour of those who attend the meetings.
- Sabha seems to have enjoys more power and the prestige.
- Sabha, Samiti and Sena were the three most important institutions in such political communities.

  Sena: all able-bodied male members.

  Samiti: all the head of families.

  Sabha: Most able, strong, learned wealthy, influential men.

Samiti was like Roman senate and Athenian Ecclesia (the periodic meeting of the Athenian citizens for conducting public business and for considering affairs proposed by the council).

Sabha and Samiti

The 'Sabha' and 'Samiti' were two different houses of assembly in the early Vedic period. The older members of the society took part in the 'Sabha' while the 'Samiti' was regarded as the common folk assembly.

---

in Ancient India, Brill, Leiden, 1968, p. 34.

TABLE 5.1 Difference between Sabha and Samiti

	Sabha	**Samiti**
Status	Aristocratic or oligarchic council	People's Assembly
Power	Had real power of governance	Had supreme formal authority but lesser or no governing powers
Membership	Limited only to few influential wealthy men	All heads of family
Size	Smaller body	Larger body
Common Membership	Sabha member might attend Samiti meetings	Samiti members could not attend Sabha meetings.
Members, Head called as	Sabhya Sabhapati	Samitiya Ishan
Chronology	Appeared before	Appeared after Sabha
Degenerated into King's court	King's parishad	Council of the Learned Pandits

5.8.4 Government of the Rajas and the Samiti

A group of monarchs or nobles, known as Rajas, reign alongside Samitis. These individuals are distinguished by their courage, oratory prowess, riches, and intelligence, rather than by being handpicked. It's possible that nobility was inherited; sons of nobles might become nobles. The college of nobles presided over the Sabha in its place. It was possibly smaller in size than the Sabha. The samiti was a separate, powerful political entity. Samiti further carried out the sacred duty of worshipping the gods in order to bestow good fortune upon the tribe as a whole. The council of nobles formed the aristocratic element, while the samiti formed the democratic. The primary duties of rulers are to protect the community from foreign assault and to ensure peace and prosperity. Under this arrangement, the government may have had a stronger sense of territorial authority over a broader area and a larger population. On becoming a Monarchy , over time, the "Chief Noble" grew too powerful and overshadowed his peers, causing Samiti to diminish to the level of a parishad. Being a chief noble or a king became inherited. The council of the king succeeded the samiti. Both the assembly (in early Rigvedic) and the assembly hall (in later Rigvedic) are referred to by the name Sabha. In ancient India, there were two people assemblies: Sabha and Samiti. They actually had a significant impact on vedic state affairs.While samiti is not mentioned in the Aitareya Brahmana, sabha occurs. An assembly known as the Samiti supported the King in ancient India. It is comparable to the Lower House or Lok Sabha of today.

Samiti has been mentioned in a number of *Rigvedic* sections, but its precise nature and purpose have not been explained. The tribe's members, known as Visha, were present at this regular assembly. The King also attended Samiti. The election of the King was one of the Samiti's most significant tasks. The Samiti's primary responsibility was to elect the king. The Samiti meetings were attended by the local chief, known as Gramini.

The Rigveda bears mention of Samiti. Samiti became more significant when the *Rigvedic* era came to an end. Sabha was little older than Samiti. The Samiti was formerly a folk assembly where people congregated to do business. Some historians claim that the Samiti was an all-inclusive assembly that comprised wealthy patrons, brahmanas, and regular people. The King served as its head. According to Arthashastra's narrative, women were also present at Samiti. The chiefs then went to Samiti as well.

A number of non-political activities were also performed by Samiti. In later Vedic times, they also talked about philosophical issues. Furthermore, religion was a factor. In order to come to a consensus, prayers were said occasionally. The fact that people's councils known as "Sabha" and "Samiti" existed and were an integral element of government provides additional proof of the Vedic age political system's growth. Numerous passages in the Rigveda mention Sabha and Samiti.

It can be inferred that the Samiti was a larger council presided over by the king where the public discussed political issues, with the participation of certain special or chosen individuals such as Brahmins and the wealthy class for administrative, political, and other purposes. Once gathered for amusement.[11]

The meaning of the Sabha appears to be both "gathered community of people" and "meeting place," its membership was restricted, and it held political power based on the descriptions found in the Rigveda. Historians have offered varying perspectives regarding the Sabha and Samiti. Aside from talks, other activities were carried out; yet, the committee is representative of an establishment with a more populous membership where political decisions were made. Regardless of the case, it is evident that both of these establishments possessed ample authority, serving as a restraint on the monarch's power. The monarch needed to maintain friendly relations with the committee (Samiti) and the parliament (sabha).

According to information acquired from later Vedic literature, Sabha and Samiti were also employed as forums for social interactions, political debates, serious debates, and gambling. "Sabhya" was the name of the sacrifice fire used during Jai Sabha sessions. Female attendees at the gathering were not included, as per the Maitrayani Samhita. The term "Sabha" is used in the same Samhita to refer to the court, and the Sahitya of Yajurveda also mentions Gramya. It is also evident from this fact that

[11] H.C. Raychaudhuri, Political History of Ancient India, Calcutta, 7th edn. 155–156. [PubMed] 41. R. Pischel and K.F. Geldner, Vedic Studies, Stuttgart, 1889–1901.

the Sabha was a functioning organization with a distinct code of conduct, as well as a defined geographical distribution of its officers and members for oversight and execution. This suggests that the assembly fulfilled its legislative duties in addition to its political ones.

After conducting a thorough investigation, V.M. Apte concludes that "on every type of policy, deliberation, decision making, and legislation were the main functions of the Committee, which was a large institution, while judicial functions mainly came under the jurisdiction of the Assembly, although it also had the right to deliberate on all political matters." This is despite the fact that it is difficult to draw any conclusions about the differences between the functions of the House and the Committee based on the evidence that is currently available.

Manusmriti states: "Sabha is the area where the learned Brahmins who are knowledgeable about the three *Vedas* sit after receiving permission from the king. Members of the Sabha should refrain from lying and defend religion against injustice. Areopagus was used by the Greeks, Curia by the Romans, and Witanagemot by the Anglo-Saxons. Similar Aryan organizations existed in India under the names Sabha and Samiti. The Sabha is often referred to as the Parishad or *Jana*ta. During the *Vedic* era, the terms Sabha Samiti and *Jana*ta were common.

There are numerous minor and large assembly forms mentioned in the writings of Brihaspati, Bhrigu, and Narada. These include moveable and immovable assemblies, rural and urban assemblies, chartered assemblies. "It seems that apart from the main assembly of the state, there were some smaller or secondary assemblies which were formed," concludes Shamashastra based on these descriptions, caste and professional assemblies, and well-organized assemblies presided over by the monarch. To address its social and political issues, each class employed. On all questions, it appears that the Pradhan Sabha held the final say.

The Sabha's membership is also referred to in a number of ways. The Sabha's other areas of concern include conflict, peace, land disputes, debt recovery, cheating in sports, inheritance, abduction of women, safety and protection of people and animals, and war. Distribution of information acquired through theft, assault, murder, and other crimes is noteworthy.

MODEL QUESTIONS FOR PRACTICE

5.1 Briefly explain the concept of Sabha and Samiti in Ancient India.

5.2 Explain the relationship between Sabha and Samiti in Ancient India.

5.3 Compare and contrast Sabha and Samiti in Ancient India

5.4 What was the role of Sabha and Samiti in Ancient India?

6

Rashtra and Rajya

6.1 UNDERSTANDING *RĀJYA* AND *RĀṢṬṚA*

The king, the minister, the country, the fortified city, the treasury, the army and the ally are the constituent elements (of the state).[1]

Kauṭiya's *Arthaśāstra*, VI.1.1

There are multiple terms in Sanskrit which are translated as state, the principal ones being *rāṣṭra* and *rājya.* Kauṭiya's *Arthaśāstra* is the earliest text to define *rājya* in terms of a political unit headed by a *rājā* (king) and consisting of seven elements which is known as *saptānga rājya.* These seven elements of the state are:

(a) *Svami* (head of the state, actually the *raja* or the head of the monarchical state)
(b) *Amatya* (the functionaries)
(c) *Janapada* (populated territory)
(d) *Durga* (fortified urban centre, usually the capital city of the realm)
(e) *Koṣa* (treasurey)
(f) *Bala* (army, if not the standing army)
(g) *Mitra* (allies).[2]

The term *rājya* received its first organized definition in Kauṭiya's *Arthaśāstra*, however, the term has its antecedents in older *Vedic* literature. The term *rājā,* is derived from the root *rañj,* which denotes someone who

[1] R.P. Kangle (tr.), *Kautiliya Arthasastra* PART II, Motilal Banarsidass, Delhi, 2010, p. 314.

[2] See R.P. Kangle ed and trn., *The Kautiliya Arthaśāstra* in three parts, Bombay, 1966–72; see the section, Prakrtisampad, Book VI.

leads or shines. Scholars suggest that according to the descriptions of *Rigveda*, it is more cogent to consider *rājā* as the leader of a clan or tribe.[3] The *Rigvedic* society being pastoral associated ownership of property with cattle and did not land; hence the epithets given to the *rājā* were terms like *gopati* (lord of cattle) or *viśpati* (lord/leader/chief of the tribe/clan) unlike the Later *Vedic rājā* is referred to as *bhupati* (lord of soil/earth), *nṛpati* (lord of men), *adhipati* (overlord).[4] The position of the *rājā* became more enhanced and powerful in the Later *Vedic* period with the settlement of the clans as sedentary residents of specified territories. The *Rigvedic viśpati* (leader of the clan) subsequently became the *viśāmattā* (the devourer of *viś* or clan) reflecting the *rājā's* power to subordinate the clan. According to Ranabir Chakravarti, "the later *Vedic* texts clearly viewed an opposition between the ruler and the vis, which was considerably subordinated. The mutually antagonistic position between the Kshatriya and the *vis* also looms large in the statement that the ruler was the deer while the vis was likened to barley; once again the juxtaposition of the devoured and the devourer is unmistakable. The exalted position of the ruler is also evident from the notion that by performing the yajnas, the ruler became Indra, Agni, Varuna and Soma. The later *Vedic* ruler was, therefore, endowed with 'occasional divinity', as Spellman suggests."[5] However, the *rājā* of the later *Vedic* texts is, like his *Rigvedic* counterpart, a leader in battle. But he is also a protector of settlements and of people, especially Brahmanas.[6] The Shatapatha and Aitareya Brahmanas refer to a kingdom of 10 generations (*dasha-purusham rajyam*). There are a few references (e.g., Atharvaveda 1.9; 3.4) to the election of the king, but these probably amounted to a ratification of hereditary succession. There is an interesting reference to the Srinjayas expelling their king Dushtaritu Paumsayana from the kingdom, in spite of his 10 generations of royal descent. This was no doubt an exception to the rule. Later *Vedic* rituals exalted the supremacy of the king, both over his kinsmen and over his people. Terms such as *samrajya* and *samrat* reflect the imperial aspirations and ambitions of certain kings.[7]

The formative period of *rājya* may therefore be traced to the Later *Vedic* period (1000–600 BCE). The nature of the political unit began to change around the 6th century BCE leading to the emergence of different kinds of political systems which included the early monarchical structure identified as *rājya* while there also formed oligarchic states known as *ganas* or *sanghas*, and tribal principalities. According to Upinder Singh, "while some communities retained their tribal character, others were making the

---

[3] Ranabir Chakravarti, *Exploring Early India* up to c. AD 1300, Macmillan, Haryana, p. 56.

[4] *Ibid.*, p. 56.

[5] *Ibid.*, p. 58.

[6] Upinder Singh, *A History of Ancient and Early Medieval India*, Pearson, p. 344.

[7] *Ibid.*, p. 344.

transition towards statehood. Larger political units were formed through the coalescing of tribes. The Purus and Bharatas came together to form the mighty Kurus, the Turvashas and Krivis formed the Panchalas, and the Kurus and Panchalas seem to have been allies or confederates."[8]

Rāṣṭṛa is an old term used frequently in the *Vedic* literature. The origin of the *rāṣṭṛa* is of particular significance as it is mentioned quite eloquently in the *Vedic* narratives. It is often mentioned that the *rāṣṭṛa* was created by sacrificial oblations after the extreme austerities undertaken by the *Vedic* seers. What was bestowed as *rāṣṭṛa* had the following attributes:

- *rāṣṭṛa* was a territory protected by the *kṣatra* or the warriors (*kṣatriyas*).
- *rāṣṭṛa* had awakened *purohitas* who were also responsible for coronating a the king and acting as advisors to him.
- The society of a *rāṣṭṛa* was organized, strongly administered and spiritually awakened.
- A historical and cultural consciousness and knowledge of the society is an apect of *rāṣṭṛa.*

The land or *bhūmi* of the *rāṣṭṛa* is perceived and invoked as mother.

According to Kauṭiya's *Arthaśāstra*, one of the seven heads of revenue collection is a *rāṣṭṛa*. The following are the heads of revenue of a rastra:

(i) *durga* (fortified urban centre)

(ii) *rāṣṭṛa* (agricultural land)

(iii) *khani* (mines and minerals)

(iv) *setu* (irrigation projects)

(v) *vana* (forests)

(vi) *vraja* (pasture grounds)

(vii) *vaṇik-patha* (trade routes).[9]

The process of development of the concept of nation and nationalism is expressed in different ways in different countries and times. The form of nation and nationalism cannot be basically the same in all the societies of the world. This stream of feeling of social unity flows in different ways in different societies. In an ethnic society, the feeling of unity of ethnicity is the essence of the nation. In a religious society, spirituality is expressed in the basic nature of the nation. In a secular society, "equality of all religions" represents the nation. But at the core of the social unity of the nation, every society has its own unique social and cultural philosophy, which works to connect diverse social classes into one thread. The validity

---

8 Ibid., p. 343.

9 See R.P. Kangle ed. and trn., *The Kautiliya Arthaśāstra* in three parts, Bombay, 1966–72; see the section, *Prakrtisampad*, Book VI.

of a nation's unity, power and ideology depends on the extent to which it succeeds in maintaining its autonomy from a dominant global ideology in any given historical context.

Monier Williams in A Sanskrit-English dictionary has given several meanings of the word Rashtra—Kingdom, Empire Country, Nation, etc. It is clear from the above facts that the word is used in a broad sense in lexical texts.

Today the word "*Rashtra*" is generally considered to be a variation of the English word "Nation" and the word "Nationality" is considered to be a variation of the English word "Nationality". Linguists believe that this word has originally evolved from the Latin word *Natus*, which means 'a race is born in which race similarity is found.' The definition of "nation" in the context of the word "Rashtra"'s usage in ancient Sanskrit literature. Indian civilization has been very ancient. The language (Sanskrit) in which Indian culture developed is considered to be the oldest language in the world. The concept of nation and nationalism is not a new thing in India. The concept of nationalism is mentioned in the oldest Indian texts.

> *The form of a nation is formed by the combination of land, people living on the land and people's culture. Land, i.e., geographical unity, people, i.e., political unity of the population, people's culture, i.e., cultural unity—the name of the combination of all three is nation. Geographical, political and cultural units are consolidated in the form of a nation.*
>
> —Sudhindra

The form of a nation mainly includes geographical, political and cultural units. According to the contraction and expansion of these three elements, the form of the nation also keeps on shrinking and expanding respectively. But mainly a nation is formed by the union of these three elements—the earth, the people living on it and its culture. Nation is not just earth, soil, mountains, rivers, etc. Their power is meaningful only when it is inhabited by the public and the power of the people is meaningful only when culture exists and develops in it. In short, it can be said that a nation is a community of people who reside on a certain territory, have their own civilization and culture and are bound by the bond of love and unity.

> *Nation is not just the name of a set of boundaries and population, it also has a specific contingency of circumstances and a specific history. A nation is like an individual.*
>
> —Nand Dulare Vajpayee

> *The form of a nation is formed by the combination of the land, the people living on the land and the culture of the people.*
>
> —Vasudevsharan Agarwal

It is clear that scholars are not unanimous about the correct meaning of the word 'nation'. They have tried to define the nation in their own ways by emphasizing on some special elements.

Nature of the Nation

In the above definitions, unity or similarity of region, caste, language, religion, culture, history, civilization, spiritual sentiments, etc. have been counted among the elements that make up the form of a nation.

1. *Nation is the people bound by the thread of ethnic unity who reside in an unbroken geographical region.*

   —Burgess

2. *'Nation' is a community of people of different occupations and social levels, irrespective of the state-related formula, who lives in a society with traditional values and common feelings, and whose every member is on the basis of language and customs. Experiences his unity with other members of the society and separateness from foreigners.*

   —German scholar Bluntschli'

3. *The organization of people or caste, which is targeted by traditional society, language, history or various political languages, is called nation.*

   —Fowler

4. *Nation is a community of people who live in a certain area and who have mutual love because of living on the same land.*

   —Barker

5. *A nation is a social group of cultural similarity which is fully conscious and determined about the unity of its mental life and expression.*

   —J.W. Garner

The use of the word "Rashtra" is visible from India's oldest literature, the Vedas. From references in Rigveda Samhita 21 and Yajurveda, it is known that the land ruled by Kshatriyas was called Rashtra.

The word "Rashtra" has been used many times in the tenth chapter of Yajurveda. 'You are the one who increases the strength and is the one who gives the nation, give him the nation' and 'You are the one who gives the nation, give me the nation'. In another mantra of Yajurveda, a desire has been expressed for the prosperity of not only all types of people but also animals and plants in the nation, which gives a comprehensive impression of the nation. In the famous Bhumisukta of Atharvaveda, there is a prayer to the land that it may establish glory and strength in our great nation. Obviously, in these prayers, that "territory" is expected from the nation, the arrangement of which is tied to a single formula. In the Rashtrabhivardhana Sukta of the Atharvaveda, there is a prayer for the king to tie the Abhivarta gem (resolution) for the growth of the nation.

This means that what the king should do for the progress and security of the nation has been explained here symbolically.

Many other words based on the word Rashtra are found in *Vedic* texts such as Rashtrakama, Abhirashtra, Rashtrabhrit, Rashtrad, Rashtriya, etc. In Nirukta, Yasaka, using the word nation, has described the unity of place and consumption of different human beings as essential for a nation. The word "Rashtra" has been used in Manusmriti, which implies the territory of a governing state whose security system is under the control of the king. The thinking about nation did not come as a result of any external thinking, but the foundation of the tradition of thinking about nation and nationality was laid by the *Vedic* sages. The *Vedic* sages not only laid the foundation but various Smritis also presented this thinking tradition in front of us in detail which became the reason for the progress of human community with the development of civilization. The discussion on nation and nationalism, which existed in the form of a seed in *Vedic* literature, flourished in Sanskrit literature and through Hindi literature became the subject of common people's mind and despite its ethnic, linguistic and religious diversities, India became a united nation.

Numerous terminology in *Vedic* literature, including Rajya, Janpad, pur, Sāmrājya, Bhaujya, Svārājya, Vairājya, Pārameṣṭhya, Māhārājya, and Rashtra, were used to designate the state. Buddhist political theories depicted states as Vijita (subjugated region), Rajja (kingdom), or Rattha (country).

Rashtra, roughly denoted people, sacred territory, a realm, dominion or jurisdiction bound by common consciousness and Dharma. Whereas nation generally denotes large groups of people claiming common bonds like Descent (ethnicity), language, religion, culture and historical identity inhabiting a particular country or territory. Word Rashtra appears for 10 times in Rigveda, whereas Rajya appears only once.

Rashtra is not a mere political entity. It transcends its physical attributes. A *Rashtra* respects pluralism and considers the entire world as a family with the mantra of *'vasudhaiva kutumbakam'* .

Rashtra of the Indic civilization is the personification of a mother and God. The Atharvaveda declares: *'mata bhumiputroahamprithvyah'*, meaning this earth is my mother and I am his son. "I am the beholder of the Rashtra," proclaims the Rigveda, "benefactors of the gods, and first among the worshipped." Rashtra was spiritual consciousness and as such is beyond the realm of mundane (routine) intellectual inquiry. *Rashtriyata* (Nationalism) was Dharma with freedom of mind, body, and spirit as well as Self-realization as its core principle. It had a divine power that does not strive to hurt or subjugate others. In the Prithvi Sukta of the Atharvaveda, there is a prayer mantra that says—"O Mother Earth, destroy those who want to subdue my Rashtra by Shastra (weapon) and/or by

Shastra (knowledge)." In different linguistic and regional culture, different words represented Rashtra; , in Bangla-'Jati', in Assamese and Odiya the word is 'Desh'; in Kannada, 'Desham'; in Tamil, 'Dessam', and 'Rashtra' in Marathi, and Gujarati.

The words Rajya, Janpad, Pur, Sāmrājya, Bhaujya, Svārājya, Vairājya, Pārameṣṭhya, Māhārājya, and Rashtra were used in *Vedic* literature to designate the state. Rattha (country), Rajja (kingdom), or Vijita (subjugated territory) were the representations of states in Buddhist political thought. The purpose of the state's founding was to put a stop to "Matsya-Nyaya," maintain law and order, and deliver justice. State power united under Dharma, the supreme ruler tying the state together, was symbolized by the term "Danda."

Organic notion of state: King, Ministers, Army, Territory, Forte, Treasury and Allies are the seven limbs of state (Arthasashtra, ManuSmriti, Mahabharata).

Important components of the Rajya/state: Fixed Territory, Sovereignty, King/Government, and the ability to establish interstate relations. State types include kingdoms, oligarchies, aristocracies, and republics.

In Buddhist Times, it seems to be an Indian fact that there is evidence in Buddhist literature that there were Panchayats even in small towns and villages of the Shakya kingdom, in which people of all classes probably got admission and the right to rule. In the literature of Buddha's time, there is often mention of a republican system of governance in which there was no hereditary ruler, the power of the state resided in the public assembly, each of whom called himself king. In the Buddhist religious text *Majjhim Nikaya, Vajji and Malla are mentioned as Ganas or Sanghas* whose rule was not in the hands of any one sovereign but in a corporate Sangha. Similarly, in Mahavastu, there is mention of 84 thousand Licchavi 'kings' who lived in Vaishali. King cannot be taken to mean a ruler here, but the meaning is definitely clear that they were all independent and powerful and together they formed a sovereign union.

6.2 NATION: MEANING AND DEFINITIONS

> *A nation is a historically constituted, stable community of people, formed on the basis of conman language, territory, economic life and psychological make-up manifested in a common culture.* —Joseph Stalin

Nation is not same as race or ethnicity; nation are abstract and imagined community, not real; nation may be multi-ethnic, multi-racial and multi-cultural. Nations not having their state: East Timorese, Kurds, Tibetans, Chechnyans Palestinians, etc. Nations may be spread into more than one state: The "Arab nation" embraces more than a dozen states, while the nation of the Kurds takes in large chunks of four states.

Multi-national states: erstwhile USSR, Yugoslavia, Czechoslovakia, and all the great empires—Mughals, Hapsburg, Ottoman, British, etc.

6.3 STATE: MEANING AND DEFINITIONS

A state is a system of relations that defines the territorial boundaries and membership of a community, binds them together in identity and cohesion, regulates its internal affairs and ensures its fair dealings with other states. The state is made up of institutions and processes that regulate various dimensions and sectors of the community and distribute various social goods according to certain principles. In terms of its basic functions, the state is the way a society controls itself by ensuring that no one else can control it. The state claims monopoly on the exercise of power. It symbolizes the centralized power that gives a few individuals the privilege to regulate and control the actions of all others.

The primary justification of the State was protection. The Manusmriti relates the following: "For, when these creatures (created by Prajāpati), being without a king, through fear, dispersed in all directions, the Lord created a king for the protection of this whole (creation)." In a later context in the same work the following is stated: "Through fear of him (the king) all created beings, both the immovable and the movable, allowed themselves to be enjoyed and swerve not from their duties." The use of punishment being thus an accepted principle with the ancient Indian political philosophers for justifying the creation of the State, we have now to see to what end it was directed. In other words, the question may be put thus: what was the object of inflicting punishment? This leads us to the antiquity of the idea of protection.

6.4 ORIGIN OF SOME CONCEPTS: EVIDENCE OF THE SATAPATHA BRAHMANA

Inter-twined to a great extent as the religious and political duties of the leaders were in the dim past, we may nevertheless endeavour to see to what extent there was any indication in the ancient texts of the future concepts which were to play an important part in the political life of the people. That the ancient Indians, even in those early days of the Vedas, the Samhitas, and the Brahmanas, were aware of important concepts relating to their socio-political life is proved by the existence of such terms like räjya, svarājya, sämrājya, bhaujya, vairājya, mahäräjya, and adhipatya which are met with, especially in the ancient texts like the Atharvaveda, the Taittiriya Samhita, the Aitareya Brahmana, and the Jaiminiya Upanişad Brahmana.

Of these terms the first is taken to mean "sovereign power", which when coupled with another term äsandi (sitting on the throne) came to be one of the characteristics of the "samrajya."

6.5 INDIAN STATE ORIGIN AND DEVELOPMENT

It would be more appropriate to use the terminology of the system. However, in contemporary political theory it is extremely difficult to separate politics from the state or the aspiration for statehood. It can even be said to be the essence of state politics.

On a practical level, the state has now become the venue of civilized civic life because 'statehood represents not only a set of institutions but also a body of rules and practices of attitudes and behaviour, which, in short, we may call citizenship, decency and let's give the name of 'civilization'. The modern state not only exercises power but also exercises power on the basis of a body of rules and regulations which are also indicators of the existence of the state.

Till now it was often believed that the nature of a state reflected the effective social and economic relations of that society. It is on the basis of this belief that there is mention of slave era states, feudal states, etc. But in contemporary literature this belief has been rejected and a state-centric model has been offered in its place. It is based on the argument that the state is not a reflection of any social or economic situation and should be understood on its own. Basically it should be understood as an autonomous institution.

The concept of the state, no matter how different its forms, often recalls the relationship of command and obedience in a social context, the effective use of power to achieve certain objectives and the efforts to establish certain structures that have existed in various historical periods may vary. But its amazing specialty can be said that it is omnipresent whether its existence is direct or symbolic. Pointing towards the omnipresence of the state, Edelman writes, "The state benefits and also frightens. Sometimes it is 'us' and often it is 'they'. It is abstract but in its name people are sent to jail, are enriched through allowances and contracts and are martyred in battle." The omnipresence of the state is such a reality of our times that neither industrialized nations, whether capitalist or socialist, nor developing nations can escape.

A political entity is one that is sovereign over a defined region, has a population living inside it, an efficient government, and the ability to interact with other states on an equal footing.

- ♦ Political community that successfully claims the monopoly of the legitimate use of physical force (violence or coercion) within a given territory, (Weber).

Kind of political subdivision of globe:

- Highest political institution of a fixed territory and population residing therein.
- Represent political independence & autonomy of people residing in a territory.
- Denote the 'body politic', politics, or 'the political'- politics is what pertains to State.

Thus State is defined as having:

- a defined territory and boarder.
- a permanent population.
- Sovereignty: both internal and external.
- an effective government.
- the capacity to enter into relations with other states.

6.6 NATION-STATE

A nation-state is a sovereign region inhabited by a single population with a shared past. There are multiple national groups present in almost every state (country) on the planet.

According to the nation-state paradigm, a population is considered to be a nation if they have common ancestry, language, and a variety of shared cultural practices.

- A state whose population considers themselves as a nation.
- When territorial boundaries of a nation is same as that of the state.
- When a nation has its own state.
- All modern states which are members of UN are considered as Nation-State.
- Emerged first in 19th and 20th Century Europe, when Linguistic and Ethnic nations got their own state.
- De-colonized states of Latin-America, Asia, and Africa were also called nation-states.
- In true sense, very few countries can be defined as Nation-State.

6.7 RASHRTA/NATION VS RAJYA/STATE

The nation-state is a political entity where the state, a centralized political organization governing a population within a territory, and the nation, a community based on a common identity, are homogenous. It is a more precise concept than "country", as a country does not require a dominant national or ethnic group.

- Political and territorial conception-political construct with elements of land, people, government and sovereignty, and abides by a Constitution.
- Sovereign political institution representing people residing in a territory.
- More tangible entity—territory, population, government, army, institutions.
- State may be multi-national.
- 'Hard' part of Nation-State.
- Older concept, existed since ancient Greek times.
- **Statism:** Doctrine that state intervention is the most appropriate means of resolving political problems, or bringing about economic and social development. State representing 'General Will' of the people and popular Sovereignty Rashtra/Nation.
- Cultural and spiritual Conception.
- Group of people claiming common descent, language, religion, culture and history and aspiring to have sovereign political formation.
- Intangible concept—imagined or abstract community.
- Nation may have multiple states.
- 'Soft' part of Nation-state.
- Nation newer concept emerged in modern Europe; Rashtra an ancient concept.
- **Nationalism:** Ideology of affection, loyalty and support to one's nation.

6.8 SAVARKAR'S CONCEPT OF HINDU RASHTRA

Sarvakar describes his idea of a "Hindu Rashtra" (Hindu Nation) as "Akhand Bharat" (Undivided India), encompassing the whole Indian subcontinent. He uses the term "Hinduism" to refer to all Indian religions. The concept of Hindu Rashtra, or Hindu Polity, was also defined by Savarkar. Hindu Polity highlighted that political and economic institutions should be founded on indigenous philosophy rather than ideas taken from the West and appealed for the preservation of Hindus and their culture.

Savarkar, who considers himself an agnostic, views Hinduism as a political and cultural identity. To the exclusion of Muslims and Christians, he frequently emphasized the social and communal cohesion between Hindus, Sikhs, Buddhists, and Jains. In his book Hindutva, Savarkar primarily argued that the Aryans who arrived in India at the beginning of time had already established a country that would later be represented by the Hindus. He said that the three foundations of their Hindutva were shared culture, ethnic characteristics, and geographic unity.

A Hindu is "primarily a citizen, either in himself or through his forefathers of 'Hindusthan,'" which is a unique geographical entity defined by mountains, oceans, and rivers. Savarkar would prefer to refer to this region as "Hindustan." In his book Hindutva: who is a Hindu (1923), Savarkar shared his conception of the Hindu Rashtra. According to Savarkar, the term "Hindutva" is a political philosophy that includes the idea of establishing Hindu hegemony in India as well as the cultural defense of Hindu nationalism. According to Savarkar's concept, the common nation (rashtra), common race (jati), and common culture or civilization (sanskriti) are the three fundamental components of Hindutva.

In his view, Hindu Rashtra is a sacred land extending from the Indus to the seas, the Himalayas to Cape Comorin. Hindus make up the majority of the population in Bharatvarsha, and Hindutva is the embodiment of their values. An essential component of Hindutva (Hinduness) is Hindu Rashtra. According to Savarkar, a Hindu is someone who considers the region from the Indus to the seas, the Himalaya to Cape Comorin—Bharatvarsha—to be their motherland or fatherland (Ptribhumi) and who is descended from Hindu parents who revered this land.

He sees three parts or components to Hindutva:

1. **Racial identity (Jati):** Due to centuries of cohabitation, Hindus have unique racial characteristics that set them apart from other races.
2. **Territorial identity:** Hindu Nation (Rashtra)—Hindus of the Bharatvarsha.
3. **Cultural identity:** A unique way of life, worldview, rituals, customs, social practices, festivals, art/craft, literature, and so on that sets Hindu nation (Hindu Rashtra) apart from Hindu State (Hindu Rajya) and can be readily differentiated from Muslim or Christian culture.

6.9 PARTHA CHATTERJEE'S INTERPRETATION OF RASHTRA

In his writings The Nation and Its Fragments: Colonial and Postcolonial Histories (1994), *Nationalist Thought and the Colonial World: A Derivative Discourse* (1993), Truths and Lies of Nationalism (2022), Indian political scientist and anthropologist Partha Chatterjee expounded on his concept of Indian nation. He distinguished between the normative grand narrative of a state's citizens being a nation and the concept of people-nation, which refers to how individuals perceive themselves as belonging to a broader group of similar individuals.

The renowned theorist Partha Chatterjee examines in this book the imaginative and potent outcomes of nationalist imagination in Asia and Africa, which is based on difference rather than identity with the nationalism that is promoted by the West. He argues that academics have misinterpreted political nationalism to mean nationalism in general and demonstrates how anticolonialist nationalists created their own sphere of sovereignty inside colonial society even before they started fighting the imperial power politically.

These nationalists distinguished between the spiritual and material realms of their culture, laying claim to the latter from the first through the representation of caste, religion, women and the family, and peasants. Chatterjee demonstrates how middle-class elites "normalized" the desires of the numerous marginal groups that characterize the spiritual realm while first imagining the country to exist in this spiritual dimension and then preparing it for political competition.

The book adds to the general theoretical discussion on nationalism and the contemporary state, even though Chatterjee uses a lot of Bengali language texts and draws her specific examples from Indian sources. The search for a postcolonial modernity is inextricably tied to earlier fights against modernity, the author concludes, after examining the ambiguities involved in first constructing a uniquely non-Western nation in the spiritual sphere and then a universalist nation-state in the material world.

He saw two grand narratives about people-nation (Hindu Rashtra and pluralist) versus multiple regional/linguistic imaginations of people-nation (Rashtra, Jati, Desham, Des, etc.) and how meaning, imagination, and consciousness of people-nation have evolved differently in different linguistic and regional cultures of India. Grand narratives about nation-states: following the path of the great empires, including the Mauryan, Gupta, Mughal, British/colonial, and postcolonial periods; these state formations were associated with hard-to-define nations. Since they both depict an integrated Indian country with several regional streams, the grand narratives of people-nation also encounter difficulties. How can the many regional conceptions of people-nations be reconciled with the Indian nation-state or the overarching story of people-nation?

Through real federalism, every people-country joins the Indian nation on an equal footing, with equal rights, recognition, and jurisdiction. In his 1983 book "Imagined Communities," Benedict Anderson (1936–2015) described a nation as an imagined community that is created through print capitalism's embrace of a mainstream culture. The British political philosopher Ernest Gellner (1925–1995) defined nationalism as "a political principle which holds that the political and the national unit should be congruent" in his 1983 book Nation and Nationalism. Nationalism gave rise to nations by symbolizing formal education systems, industrialization, urbanization, and cultural homogenization. The nation is defined as "a named population sharing a historic territory, common myths and historical memories, a mass public culture, a common economy, and common legal rights and duties for its members" by Anthony D. Smith (1939–2016).

6.10 A.S. ALTEKAR'S CONCEPT OF RASHTRA-RAJYA

The Sanskrit word for "nation" is Rashtra. Rashtra has an adjectival form called Rashtriya. The word "rashtra" combines the concepts of the state and the country (Rajya). In a sense, the state represents the nation, just as the nation is represented by the state. Since the English term "nation-state" and the Hindi word "rashtra" are essentially comparable today, it is clear that the Indian state of Maharashtra has only existed as a nation-state since the mid-1900s.

Charvak indicates that India as a nation is the result of multiple ideological investments, political maneuvers, and administrative agreements that create a fiction of continuity for their own justification by detailing the accidents of its colonial and postcolonial history. How a national people's federation could and ought to be envisioned for the Indian nation. Without a doubt, the Indian people are found throughout the nation.

People have created their own conceptions of it in each section via shared identities and values, lived experiences, and group battles. A just, equitable, and useful society can be achieved by giving equal weight to all these claims over hypothetical but historically actualized communal lives within a decentralized federal system. It is necessary to view diversity as the strongest sign of unity rather than the catchphrase "unity in diversity."

Fantastic works of speculative fiction might be created from the wish to have an old nation. Were the Muaryas, Guptas, Delhi Sultanate, Vijaynagara, Mugals, and Marathas empires not considered major states? They most definitely were. However, they weren't nations; they were empires. It's also possible that just recently has global awareness of popular sovereignty and self-determination grown.[10]

The origin of the state is a topic that is covered in great detail in contemporary political publications. There are sporadic conjectures on the state's genesis in the Mahabharata and the Diggha Nikaya. Despite their divergent historical and religious contexts, these writings exhibit a notable degree of parallelism. The state may only be a pale replica of the ideal one that Plato defined in his Republic, which is likely to be seen as the idealization of such a Golden Age.

The Mahabharata continues by saying that for a considerable amount of time, society prospered without a monarchy or judicial system, but that eventually, there was a moral decline. Humanity descended into immorality

[10] Partha Chatterjee, *All Nations are Modern in the Truth and Lies of Nationalism: As Narrated by Charvak*, Permanent Black, 2021, pp. 5–25.

as cupidity, greed, and selfishness took hold of their minds and turned society into a literal hell. The rule of the jungle started to take effect; just as it always does among fish, the strong ate the weak (Matsya-Nyaya). In the Mahabharata, it is implied that people voted Virajas as king; however, the Digha Nikaya explicitly says that once Mahajanasammata granted the people's wish to eliminate chaos, they elected him as their king.[11]

Contemporary writers have advanced a number of other ideas regarding the genesis of the state. There is a claim that in the distant past, people voluntarily gave a person authority over governance, either because the person was a priest who could guarantee heavenly assistance and favors, a magician who could call for rain, or a physician who could heal patients. It's probable that the patriarchal joint family system originated as a seed from which the state eventually developed.[12]

Comparative philology's data demonstrates that the Aryans lived in joint households with their grandparents, father, uncles, nephews, sons, and daughters-in-law even when they were in their original home. These joint families occasionally numbered two or three hundred members, according to Homer's testimony.[13]

The joint family's patriarch had extensive control over all of its members. According to the *Rigvedic* evidence, families, ianmans, visas, and janas made up the early Aryan civilization. Janmans appear to have correlated with a village made up of individuals asserting a shared ancestry, and several such villages bound by familial ties appear to have formed a vis: its head was referred to as a Vispati. Visas were closely allied, and in the field of combat, battalions were frequently organized according to the vis from whence they were recruited. (Ṛigveda, X,84,4)[14]

The Rigveda (c. 2500 B.C.) makes repeated references to certain tribes, such as the Yadus, Purus, Anus, Turvasas, etc., in addition to vispatis and janapatis. It is stated that the Bharata people were shielded by Visvamitra's prayers. In contrast, the idea of Rashtra or a territorial state was gradually developing in the later *Vedic* era; this is seen in the Atharvaveda. The Taittriya Samhita mentions a ceremony that, if partially carried out, may provide a king overlordship over his tribe (vis), but not over the entire nation (Rashtra).

The Brahmana literature often describes the emperor as the ruler over the entire world, bounded by the sea, rather than only over all the tribes. It is evident that at this point, the nation of a territorial state was completely created.[15]

---

[11] A.S. Altekar, *Origin and Types of the State in State and Government in ancient India*, Motilal Banarsidass, Banaras, 1949, p. 16.

[12] *Ibid*. p. 17.

[13] *Ibid*. pp. 17–18

[14] *Ibid*. p. 18.

[15] *Ibid*. 18

MODEL QUESTION FOR PRACTICE

6.1 Discuss the similarities and differences between the concept of 'Rashtra' and 'Rajya'

6.2 Discuss the evolution of Rashtra (Nation) and Rajya (State) in Ancient India Political Thought.

6.3 Define Savarkar's concept of Hindu Rashtra.

6.4 Define the Partha Chatterjee's interpretation on Rashtra.

6.5 Explian the A.S. Altekar's concept of Rashtra-Rajya.

7

Jati and Varna

7.1 HISTORICAL EVOLUTION OF JATI AND VARNA

Jāti, or caste, and varna, or theoretical classification based on occupation, are two different ideas. The term "community" (jāti) describes the hundreds of endogamous communities that are found all throughout the subcontinent. Based on the same gotras, a jati can be split up into exogamous groupings. Jatis were formed by society. Discrimination among people led to the creation of the caste system. The caste system was first established in the kingdom according to the occupations of its citizens. Eventually on, it transformed into the home of the birth. Although the exact history of the caste system in India and Nepal is unknown, it appears to have started more than 2,000 years ago. This system, linked to Hinduism, classified people according to their professions. Caste was formerly based on a person's employment, but it quickly became inherited. In the past, a person's aptitude and attributes were used to determine their Varna. The caste system was not inflexible in the early Vedic era. Later in the Vedic era, however, Varnas were assigned according to birth. As a result, Varnas changed in later Vedic times according to the caste system's inheritance. The Vedic period, which lasted from around 1500 to 1000 BCE, saw the implementation and acknowledgement of the caste system in ancient India. In order to create eternal order, maintain the purity of a caste, and free individuals from burdensome obligations, people were divided into groups according to their Varna.

The most peculiar characteristic of the Hindu society is the system called varna and jati. Varna is caste on the bases of position in the society and jati a sub-caste (Varna in Sanskrit actually means colour). Varna is the positional label imposed on different castes as a yardstrick for social classification. It was this discrimination, exploitation and human rights violations on the basis of the varna-jati classification that the reformist movements opposed the most. The varnas are four in number : Brahamanas, Kshatriya as, Vaishyas and Shudras. And thus the Brahamana who were the custodians of the worship of gods and the performance of the rituals were sanctioned the highest of varnas. The Shudras who were allotted the manual labour and related 'clean' jobs the lowest. Below these four layers were the numerous othe castes and sub-castes engaged in 'unclean' job. These people are outside the varna system and were historically treated as 'untouchable,' a practice now prohibited by law but still persisting in some parts of the country. Mahatma Gandhi referred to them as harijans, meaning 'people of Lord Vishnu.' They now call themselves dalits. The government has designated them as scheduled tribes.

'Varna' did not have any particular use in the operations of the social system, nor had it a built-in power for that. But the most important factor was the caste or jati. Jati denoted a particular community with a definition on customs by the large, having a particular profession hereditarily and inclusive marriage rights. Each varna would contain several jatis each of which had its own customs and practices.

Historian Romila Thapar writes on the genesis and formulation of the caste system: when the Aryans first came to India they were divided into three social classes, the warrior or aristocracy, the priests, and the common people. There was no consciousness of caste, as evidenced by remarks such as "a bard am I, my father is a leech, and my mother grinds corn." Professions were not hereditary, nor were there rules limiting marriages within these classes or taboos on who one could eat with. The three divisions merely facilitated social and economic organizations. The first in direction of castes (as distinct from class) was taken when the Aryans treated the dasas (slaves) as belong the social pale, probably owning to a fear of the dasa and the even greater fear that assimilation with they would lead to a loss of Aryan identity. Ostensibly the distinction was largely that of colour the dasas being darker and of an alien culture. The terms varna (theoretical classification based on occupation) and jati (caste) are two distinct concept. Jati (community) refers to the thousands of endogamous groups prevalent across the subcontinent. A jati may be divided into exogamous groups based on the same gotras.

To understand the process of social stratification in early India, it is necessary to understand the nature of varna and caste. Varna and caste are basically of the same type. Society has been divided into four categories through the Chaturvarnya system. Different duties have been prescribed for Brahmins, Kshatriyas, Vaishyas and Shudras, but in terms of social status and purity, Brahmins have been given the first place, Kshatriyas second, Vaishyas third and Shudras fourth.

There are only four varnas but the number of castes is in thousands. According to the 1901 census, there were only 2,000 types of Brahmins in Bharatvarsh. These thousands of castes are included in one or the other varna and from the point of view of ritual, attention is also paid to their mutual cleanliness. Both varna and caste are genetic, and restrictions regarding marriage and food apply to both. Daughter and breed are considered the basis of both varna and caste. Caste means birth. Therefore, caste is determined by birth, not by deeds; the same thing applies in determining varna.

Initially varna was considered a large unit and there could be several castes within one varna. As the number of castes increased due to the inclusion of foreigners and tribes in the varna-divided society, the theory of varnasankara or varnasankarin continued to be propounded in the religious scriptures to justify their existence. Most of the castes were described as Varnasankar or Varnasankirna and it was said that these castes were mostly born due to inverse relationship. When a woman of a higher caste is related to a man of a lower caste, then such relationship is called *Pratiloma*. For example, due to the union of a Shudra man with a Brahmin woman, *Pratiloma* child Chandal is born. *Anuloma* relation is the opposite.[1]

A man of a higher caste marries a woman of a lower caste. In this way, if a Shudra woman has a child from a Brahmin man, it will be Anuloma, and will be called Nishad. It will be further explained that the theory of hybridity has been coined, there is little to no reality in this theory. The number of varnas is still considered to be basically four, but with the advent of the medieval period, the distinction between varna and caste started disappearing. There are descriptions of many such villages which have been described as villages of 36 varnas. This means that 36 types of castes lived in them. So actually there is not much difference between castes. Stratification of Indian society happened due to caste discrimination. We have to find out how cast and casteism arose and how they changed with changes in society. Some people are of the opinion that Indian society has been based on caste system since ancient times and recently it has started changing due to the pressure of industrialization. Western Indologists have described it as a rigid, dormant and unchanging society.

Restrictions on marriage and social interaction, heredity and hierarchy are the main features of the caste system considered to be immutable. Members of a caste can neither have marital relations outside their own caste nor can they take food from the lower caste. High—The feeling of inferiority is linked to birth and heredity. Only by being born as a Brahmin, one cannot change one's varna during one's lifetime. Castes come under one or the other category and in terms of rituals, Brahmins are in the highest rank and Kshatriyas are in the second category. In Buddhist texts, Kshatriyas get the first place and Brahmins get the second place, and the basis of varna is the place of birth.

---

1 Ram Sharan Sharma, *Economic and social history of early India*, Hindi Medium implementation Directorate, New Delhi, 2011, pp. 43–45.

7.2 INTRODUCTION OF VARNA AND JATI

The two terms class and Varna are the primary indicators of the class structure that forms the basis of traditional Indian life. "Varna" denotes a newborn's inherited roots; it indicates color, type, nature, and quality. "Jati" is the second term, which refers to the form of existence determined by birth. Most people attribute the idea to a passage in the Rigveda called *Purusha Sukta.* A frequently referenced source is the Manusmriti's commentary on the Varna system. In opposition to these literate categorizations, numerous Hindu scriptures and teachings contest and the Varna system of social stratification. The root *vṛ* is the source of the Sanskrit word varna, which means "to cover, to envelop, count, classify, consider, describe, or choose." "Colour, outward appearance, exterior, form, figure, or shape" is the definition of the word as it appears in the Rigveda. According to the Mahabharata, the term signifies "color, tint, dye, or pigment. "Certain Vedic and medieval sources define Varna as the "color, race, tribe, species, kind, sort, nature, character, quality, or property" of an object or people. In the Manusmriti, "Varna" refers to four social classes. The Dharmashastra literature, the Mahabharata, and the Puranas all describe the varna divide in the post-Vedic era. The Dharmashastras contain a thorough discussion of the varna system. Dharmashastras' Varna system separates people into four groups: Brahmins, Kshatriyas, Vaishyas, and Shudras. According to the Chandogya Upanishad, a person's Varna is determined by their birth and past births: The Varna system in South Asia is mentioned in ancient Buddhist scriptures, but the specifics imply that it was flexible, non-rigid, and devoid of elements of a social stratification structure. The first written account of Varna and Jati in Jain literature is found in Jinasena's eighth-century Jain work, Ādi purāṇa. The connection between varna and jati is also covered in the literature Adi Purana. Sikhism is a late 15th-century religion that has its roots in the Indian subcontinent's Punjab region. Sikh scriptures refer to Jati as Zat or Zat-biradari and Varna as Varan. The puranic speculation establishes causal connection between the rise of Varna and the origin of state.[2]

As per Dipankar Gupta—'From Varna to Jati: The Indian caste system, from the Asiatic to the feudal mode of production, Varna was manifestation of Asiatic mode of production characterising general exploitation; agricultural operations were open to all categories of the varna scheme, tile lower orders were quite self-sufficient and this precluded any clear demarcation between peasants and artisan. Jati was the result of Feudal mode production which characterized by localized exploitation in a closed village; now each village community was doing a specific job and Jajmani system developed.

[2] Ram Sharan Sharma, *Aspects of Political Ideas and Institutions in Ancient India,* Motilal Banarsidass Publishers Private Ltd, 2001. pp. 233.

TABLE: 7.1 Thinkers and their perspectives on Caste System

M.N. Srinivas (1916–1999) an Indian sociologist and social anthropologist; wrote 'Caste in Modern India' and 'The Dominant Caste'; gave the concept of 'Sankritization' to denote social mobility of castes.

Rajni Kothari (1928–2015) an Indian political scientist; known for his formulation of the Congress system; wrote 'Politics in India(1970)'; discussed politicisation of caste and caste in politics.

Dipankar Gupta (1949) is an Indian sociologist; wrote 'From Varna to Jati: The Indian caste system, from the Asiatic to the feudal mode of production'; explained Varna and Jati from Marxist perspective.

Nicholas B. Dirks (1947) American academic and the former Chancellor of the University of California, Berkeley; wrote 'Castes of Mind: Colonialism and the Making of Modern India (2001)'; explained how Indian Caste system was substantiated by Census and Governability of the colonial masters.

Traditional Indian life is primarily based on a system of class division which is denoted by two terms varna (colour, character, nature and quality) (M. Williams) and jati (the form of existence fixed by birth) (Apte).

The Indian people are thus broadly divided into four groups

- The Brahmanas or the priestly class.
- The Ksatriyas or the knightly order.
- The Vaisyas or the businessmen and traders.
- The Sudras or the class that served the others.

In the famous Purusa-Sukta occurring in the Tenth Mandala of the Rigveda explains:

- The Brahmana was his mouth.
- The Rajanya was made his arma.
- The Vaisyas constituted his thighs.
- The Sudras sprang from his feet.

The so-called fourfold caste system as we find it in India was invented in the later Rigvedic age. In ancient Iran this fourfold division was not based on birth. Some scholars hold that though the second, third and fourth groups (Rathestas, Vastria Fxhouyania and Huiti) did not form any caste groups. In its early stage in India also the fourfold division of mankind was possibly not a hereditary institution but based on guna and karma as some of the later authorities assert. Thus the Lord declares in the Gita, "The fourfold order was created by Me according to the division of quality and active function". Again, "The works of Brahmanas, Ksatriyas,

Vaisyas and Sudras are divided according to the qualities (gunas) born of their own inner nature".

7.3 MEANING AND SIGNIFICANCE OF CHATURVARNAS AND CHATURAASHRAM IN ANCIENT INDIA

Brahmin, Kshatriya, Vaishya, and Sudra are the four varnas that are first mentioned in the Purusha-sukta of the Rigveda. The oldest written record ever discovered. Sixteen verses of the Rigveda's 10th mandala's sukta depict the purusha, the cosmic being, in its enormous form (virat swaroop). According to several academics, these are interpolarations when contrasted to the family mandalas (second through seventh) of the Rigveda. This specific verse merely states that the brahmans, kshtriyas, Vaishyas, and Shudras originated from the purusha's mouth, two arms, two thighs, and two feet, respectively. As there was no established caste structure, this divide was made according to work rather than birth. Systems were developing in an effort to make society more organised as it was growing, expanding, and becoming more complex. The aashrama system split life into four segments based on the idea that each person would live for 100 years. Studying and developing one's skills took up the first 25 years of celibacy practise and student life (brahmcharyaashrama). In the following 25 years of a householder's life (grihasthaashram), one began to make money, got married, had kids, and raised them well. In order to live a pious life of spirituality and avoid interfering with his children's lives after fifty years, when the children had grown up, the man was obliged to relocate to the forest encircling woodland abode (vaanaprasthaashram). The final 25 years of samnyaasaashrama were spent renunciating, moving to a more remote area of the forest, engaging in higher spiritual practises, and becoming ready to unite with God. These aashrama lifestyles included doing yagnas.

Vedic scholars were assigned to study the four-fold varna system constantly. The notion of divinity and social divide came from the theory's beginning. The essentiality of division for the accomplishment of the work was reflected in both Vedic and Post-Vedic civilization. Actually, in terms of the distribution of work, it appears to be true. However, the effort and virtue of the potential capacity are only fixed by birth identification.

The Indian people are thus divided into four groups:

- Brahmanas/The priesty class
- The Kshatriyas/The knighty order
- The Vaishyas/The husbandmen and traders
- The Shudras (labourers, the class that served the others).

7.4 EVOLUTION OF VARNA (JATI)

Around 1500 BC, the arrival of the Aryans led to the widespread adoption of the varna system in India. These people were immigrants who moved to India from the Central Asian region. The late Vedic society gave rise to the varnas. While the Shudras are presumably a Brahmanical invention from northern India, the first three groups—the Brahmins, Kshatriyas, and Vaishyas—have similarities with other Indo-European communities. In Hinduism, varṇa denotes a social class inside a conventional hierarchical Hindu society. Texts such as the Manusmriti, which identify and categorize four varnas and prescribe their vocations, obligations, and responsibilities, or Dharma, serve as prime examples of the doctrine. A group is called a varana in Sanskrit. The ancient Indian society was split into four groups with the arrival of the Aryans: Brahmin, Kshatriya, Vaishya, and Shudra. The Varna System in Hinduism was founded on guna, yoga, class, and colour.

Introduction

- **Varna:** It contextually means "colour, race, tribe, species, kind, sort, character, quality, property" of an object or people in some vedic and medival texts.
- The first mention of varna is found in *Purusha Suktam* verse of ancient Sanskrit Rigveda.
- According to it, there are four varnas, Brahmins, Kshatriyas, Vaishyas and Shudra
- The Aryans of India might have brought this from outside.
- As per the Rigveda, the Aryans were group immigrants who were white-skinned people. The ultimate motive of Aryans was to enslave the black-skinned by suppression.
- These local natives who were suppressed and opposed by Aryans were known as "Shudras". Shudras were called outcasts by upper three levels of people.
- They were forced to choose occupations such as cleaning pollutants and maintaining sanitary system of society. They were termed as the untouchables.

7.5 DIFFERENCE BETWEEN VARNA SYSTEM AND JATI OR CASTE SYSTEM

Varna system was based on work of people but eventually time to time it changes into caste system that is based on birth. The caste system originated from the division of society into specific roles and responsibilities based on birth. For example, if someone was born into a Brahmin family, they were typically assigned roles and duties associated with the Brahmin caste. This practice established the caste system, where social status and duties were determined by one's birth.

- The Gita was being composed about 200 B.C., the early Dharmasutra writers had been strongly advocating that the four-fold division was primarily based on birth. This writing illustrate how the varna gradually turn into jati.
- The varna system was not, however, dying out completely. Dr. D.R. Bhandarkar has shown now in the historical period various foreign tribes, who entered into India, were admitted into castefold. This was possible only through the operation of the varna system which is elucidated in pages of later works.
- In the same epic we found that by means of good deeds a sudra can be a Brahmana and a Vaisaya a Ksatriya. Even in Harivamsa informs that two sons of Nabhagaristha who were vaisyas became Brahmanas.
- Thus we find that both the varna and the Jati theories are operating simultaneously in the ancient period.

Brhama Purana

- The Brahma Purana is one of the eighteenth major Purana collection of Hindu texts in Sanskrit language. It is listed as the first Maha-Purana in all the anthologies and therefore also called Adi-Purana.
- Another title of this text is the Saura Purana, because it includes many chapters related to surya as the Sun God.
- Vyasa had written the Brahma Puranam which concludes of 18,000 verses.
- The Brahma Purana manuscripts are encyclopedia in their coverage, such as Cosmogony, Sanskara, Genealogy (chapters of Ethics and duties), Administration, Diplomacy, Trade, Geography, etc.

The Adi Purana, or primary Purana, mothers of all later Puranas, constituted the fifth Veda compiled by Ved Vyasa as it is presented Vedic ideas in story.

- However, historians trace the rise of Puranic literature from 5th century onwards, that tells the story of pilgrim spots, as well as Jati Purana that even tell us about the different kind of castes.
- In this text, tell us about inter-marriage caste is result of loss of purity, e.g., marriage between a Nishada (born of Brahim father and a Shudra mothers) and a Vaidehaka mothers (born of Vaishya father and Brahmin mother). A son born of a Brahman mother by a Kshatriya father is called a Suta, while a son begotten by a Vaishya father on a Brahmani woman, is called as Vaidehaka.

- In other narratives, the community self-identified itself as a kings of the chavar dynasty, who lost their status, because they broke the rules of rituals purity in a crisis.
- Jati Purana are written in local languages, and many exist purely in oral forms, some are meant to keep people in their place and others are meant to give a higher status to a caste or justify its profession, or simply work aside.
- Again in such a Kalika Purana, we find the story of how Parshurama killed the all Kshatriya on earth, but spared their unborn children, and provided they were not raised to be a warriors.
- The children decided to invoke Shiva and ask them right to use weapons. But Saraswati invoked by Parsurama twisted their tounge and they said may we become traders. This is the caste story of coppersmiths. Thus, the community sees itself as primarily Kshatriya, but forced by a twist of fate to be Vaishyas.

7.6 VARNA VS JATI

The word "Vri," which refers to one's profession choice, is the root of the name "Varna". Varna is therefore associated with a single hue or color combination. Conversely, the term "Jana," which denotes giving birth, is the root of the word "caste," or jati. Caste is therefore a matter of birth. The Rigveda, the oldest extant Indian scripture, contains a song that describes the varnas as the Brahman (priest), Kshatriya (noble), Vaishya (commoner), and Shudra (servant) that emanated from the mouth, arms, thighs, and feet of the primordial person (purusha) at the time of creation. The term Jati comes from the Sanskrit word jāta, which means "born or brought into existence". Although the phrase is most frequently used to refer to a person's caste, which is established the moment they are born, it can also refer to other associations, such as linguistic and religious groupings. There is not a single recognized approach in India for classifying the approximately 3,000 jatis in existence into hierarchical hierarchy. Jati rating, however, is a local concept that is highly tied to pollution and purity in each place. Not every jati does their specific task; each jati has a different job to do.

Varna

- Four division of society based on personal aptitude, qualities and social needs.
- Only 4 varnas.
- Initially not hereditary.
- Different Jati seems to have originated from intermixing of varnas through Hypergamy/Hypogamy.

- More ritual and spiritual based.
- More theoretical or bookish concept/framework.

Jati

- Localized birth based social groups associated with same occupation and having specific characteristics.
- Thousands of Jati.
- Heriditary.
- Localised/regional social systems.
- Each jati traces its association to one of the varna.
- More temporal, mundane and socio-economical system.
- Real and practical—affect daily life of people.
- Distinction in custom, dress and speech.
- Disabilities and privileges enjoyed by different Jati.
- Regional and local variations in Jati system.
- Graded inequality.
- Religious sanction.
- Jati may have multiple connotations: for many people it also denoted nation (Rashtra).

The terms varna (theoretical classification based on occupation) and jāti (caste) are two distinct concepts. Jāti (community) refers to the thousands of endogamous groups prevalent across the subcontinent. A jati may be divided into exogamous groups based on the same gotras. The classical authors scarcely speak of anything other than the varnas; even Indologists sometimes confuse the two.

Jāti is the term traditionally used to describe a cohesive group of people in the Indian subcontinent, like a tribe, community, clan, sub-clan, or a religious sect. Each Jāti typically has an association with an occupation, geography or tribe. Different religious beliefs (e.g., Sri Vaishnavism or Smarthism or Shaivism) or linguistic groupings may also define some Jātis. The term is often translated approximately in English as *caste*.

There is a clear difference between Varna and Jati concept. It is true that caste and creed are related to each other in social status, but on other grounds we can easily separate them from each other. Varna is a division of society based on occupation while 'Jati' is a division that was not restricted to only case on 'varna' system. It is a division based on birth units of Hindu society.

There are only four varnas but there are thousands of Jati; The four varnas are 'Brahmins', 'Kshatriyas', 'Vaishyas' and 'Shudra'.

According to the Vedas, consistent encroachment on other life responsibilities engenders and unstable society. Brahmins, Kshatriyas,

Vanish and Shudras form the fourfold nature of society, each assigned appropriate life duties and ideal disposition. Men of the first three hierarchical castes are called the twice born; first, born of their parents, and second of their guru after the sacred thread initiation they wear over their shoulder.

7.7 FOUR VARNA IN INDIAN SOCIETY

The varna system is seemingly embryonic in the Vedas, later elaborated and amended in the Upanishads and Dharmashastras:

1. **Brahmins:** Yajna, teaching, studies, and religious rituals and practices are known as Brahmins; Brahmins have a special plane in society. Brahmins were revered as an incarnation of knowledge itself, enclosed with the precepts and sermons to be discharged to all varnas of society. Priests, gurus, rishis, teachers and scholars constituted the Brahmins community. However, anyone from other varnas could also become a Brahmin often expensive acquisition of knowlwdge and cultivation of one's intellect. By the means of good deeds a shudra can be a Brahmana and a vaisya a Kshatriya. The Harivamsa informs us that two sons of Nabhagaristha who were vaisyas become Brahmanas. All Brahmin mens were allowed to marry women of the first three Varnas, whereas marrying a shudra woman would, be marginally, bereft the Brahmin of his priestly Status. Neventhless, a shudra woman would not be rejected if the Brahmin consented. As per Manusmriti, a Brahmin woman must only marry a Brahmin and no other, but she remains free to choose the man. She, under rare circumstances is allowed to marry a Kshatriyas or a Vaishya, but marrying a shudra man is restricted. The restrictions in inter-caste marriage are to avoid subsequent inpurity of progeny born of the matches.
2. **Kshatriya:** After the Brahmins the Kshatriyas were replaced. The place of arms in the body was the same as that of Kshatriyas in society. Kshatriyas constituted the warrior clan, the kings, rulers of territories, administrative, etc. All Kshatriyas would be sent to a Brahmins's ashram from an early age until they became wholly equipped with requisite knowledge. They were allowed to may a woman of all varnas with mutual consent. Although a Kshatriyas or a Brahmin woman would be the first choice, Shudra women were not barred from marrying a Kshatriya. Kshatriya women, like their male counterparts, were trained in martial disciplines, well-versed in warfare, had the right to perform duties in the king's absence, and were involved in the affairs of the kingdom. We read in the Talagunda inscription how Brahmanas Mayurasarman

took up the sword to conquer the earth and his descendents took the title of varman, a Kshatriya title, acoording to manu, i.e., they became Kshatriyas.

3. **Vaishyas:** Vaishya is the third varna in society often Brahmins and Kshatriyas, represented by agriculturalists, traders, money lenders, and those involved in commerce. Vaishyas are also the twice-born and go to the Brahmins Ashram to learn the rules of a virtuous life and to refrain from intentional or accidental misconduct. Vaishyas women also supported their husbands in business, cattle rearing, and agriculture. They were equally free to choose a spouse of their choice from the four varnas.
4. **Shudras:** The last varna represent the backbone of a properous economy. Shudras were the lowest caste in society, they were called legs in the body. Shudras were powerless, to serve all upper classes, Shudras are the most varied since there seemingly are more restrictions on them. However, Atharvaveda allows Shudras to hear and learn the vedas by heart and the Mahabharata, too; supports the inclusion of Shudras in ashram and their learning of the vedas. Shudras are not the twice-born, hence not required to wear sacred thread like the other varnas. A Shudra man was only allowed to marry a Shudra woman, but a Shudra woman was allowed to marry a man from any of the four varnas.

7.8 ORIGIN OF VARNA SYSTEM IN INDIA

The first mention of Varna is found in the famous "Purush Suktam" occurring in the tenth Mandala of the Rigveda:

"The Brahmana was his mouth; The Rajanya was made his arm; The Vaisyas constituted his thighs; The Sudras sprang from his feet".

The context of the origin of different organs is related to their work. The origin of Brahman from the mouth is related to the work of study and teaching. Such as the act of speaking and it also demonstrated the Society's excellence. The Kshatriyas is said to be form the arm due to the task of hand defence. The vaisya is said to be Jangha, as it works to support the body, So the work of the world is to help Society through production. Shudra's position is like that of feet, which perform the work of labour but do not get its fruits.

According to Avesta (The primary collection of religious text of Zoroastrianism composed in the Avestan language) the ancient Iranian people were also divided into an analogous division, viz., the Atharvas (priests), Rathestas or charioteers (The chief of warrior), Vastriya Fshouyanta (agriculturists and artisans) and Hiuti (the Sents). It is also mentioned in the peace festival of the Mahabharata.

This shows that the system of division of mankind into four groups developed among the different branches of Indo-Iranians and had there been direct evidences we could have conclude that the Aryans of India might have brought it from the outside.

Thus it has been considered the so-called fourfold caste system as we find it in India was invented in the lated Rigvedic age.

7.9 ORIGIN OF JATI (CASTE SYSTEM) IN INDIA

Indian Society is identify on the basis of Jati Caste is the most important element in today's society and polities, the Jati system today cannot be understood without the concept of electoral politics. Even though the caste system is criticized, the role of caste in Indian politics is clear, from voting to the formation of the cabinet. Jati is a hierarchical system in which stratification and found. The origin of caste among scholars has led to different opinions about their role in Indian society. Some scholars support the origin of Jati in the caste system itself. The question arises whether the caste system existed even in the ancient times, had any role in society and politics and can be analysed on the basis of the available literary sources.

Jati

The census report shows that the existence of at least three thousand caste rapidly exclusive in marriage and dinning and each claming superiority in marriage and dining over the ohers.

Anthropologists thinks that this multiplicity is due to the following factors:

(a) The rise of various functional groups that acquired hereditary characters and followed the laws of endogamy and exogamyly carpeners, potters, goldsmiths, blacksmiths, etc.

(b) The rise of race caste occasioned by the entrance of tribal groups in the Brahmanical society.

(c) The emergence of Sectarian caste, e.g., the Lingayats and Vanisnava caste in Mahabhartha, etc.

(d) Other factors, e.g., migration, cross-breeding, etc.

It is difficult to determine whether there was ansectarian caste before or during the time of Yajnavalkya. The other three processes of such a rise of mixed caste what would be the position of people like Vishvamitra and others who had acquired Bharhamahood not by their birth but by their deeds. As we have already seen Harivamsa refers to Nabhagaristha's two sons who were vaisyas but later on become Brahmanas. We read in the Talagunda inscription how Brahman Mayurasarman took up sword to conquer the earth and his descendants took the title of varham, a Kshatriya title according to Manu, i.e., they become Kashatriya.

Yajnavalkya holds that the blameless marriage of the parents was the pre-condition of the birth of a Sajati. Balam Bhatta here raised that interesting question of niyoga, declaration legal by Yanjavalkya himself, and observed that "the son raised on a Brahama widow by her husband's younger brother by the method of niyoga is also a Brahamana, through the parties in this case are not married to each other this is the case of a sastra created Brahamana".

The presence of numerous caste groups in ancient India society and the number of sub-caste are multiplying everyday. The earlier Census report shows the existence of at least three thousand.

Manu refers to six *anuloma* castes but actually names three only are:

1. Ambasiha
2. Nisada
3. Ugra

Manu's enumeration only three name shows that he was not sure, as it has already been started before, regarding the status of the issues of a man of the higher caste with a woman of the immediate next order.

7.10 THEORIES OF JATI IN INDIA

The following are some of the major theories about the origins of Jati (caste) in India are:

7.10.1 Traditional Theory

The traditional wisdom maintains that the Jati system has divine beginnings and that the four varnas of the varna system descended from the body of Brahma. Thus, the caste system is an extension of this structure. The Brahmins, who comprised the head of Brahma and were usually teachers and thinkers, stood at the top of the hierarchy. Brahma's arms were used to make Kshatriyas, warriors and kings; his thighs were used to make Vaishyas, or merchants; and his feet were used to make Shudras, or lower castes. That is, the shudra's function is to serve everyone else, since the arms provide protection, the thighs enable farming or trade, and the feet support the entire body. This viewpoint's proponents use passages from the Rigveda such as Purushasukta and Manusmiti to support their claim.

7.10.2 Breed-based Theory

In Sanskrit, jati is known as varna, which means color. It was the Chaturvarna system that gave rise to "Brahmins, kyshrtiya, Vaishyas, and Shudras" and ultimately to the caste system in Indian civilization. In "Races and Culture in India," Indian historian D.N. Majumdar claims that the caste system began in India after the arrival of the Aryans.

The Rigvedic literature emphasizes how Aryans and non-Aryans differ from one another in terms of speech, religious practices, physical characteristics, and skin color. The main basis for the varna system that prevailed during the Vedic period was the division of labor and profession. In the Rigveda, the three classes Brahman, Kshatra, and Vis are referenced several times. Brahma and the poet-priest represented the warrior chief and Kshatra, respectively. Vis is made up of all regular people. The Rigveda makes only one reference to the fourth class, known as the "Shudra," who were primarily domestic workers.

7.10.3 Political Theory

This argument argues that Brahmins invented the caste system as a clever ploy to gain power and prominence in society. According to Dr. Ghuraye, "Jati, a Brahmanical descendant of Indo-Aryan culture, grew up in the Ganga and later migrated to other regions of India." Furthermore, in order to win the king's favor and obtain spiritual merit through a priest, the Brahmins integrated this principle.

7.10.4 Professional Theory

Within Jati, there is a hierarchy based on occupation. People who worked for dirty corporations were thought to have noble and superior jobs. According to Newfield's theory, labor and function were the only factors in the creation of the caste system in India. Occupational divergence and the creation of many subspecies, such as Teli, Chamaras, and Blacksmiths, coincided with functional development.

7.10.5 Development Theory

This hypothesis holds that there is no specific date when the caste system originated. It is the outcome of a protracted social development process.

1. Business run by families.
2. Purity is something that Brahmins value.
3. The caste system's origins are also explained by the "Karma" and "Dharma" philosophies.
4. There is a lack of strict, unitary authority over the state.
5. Rules are reluctant to enforce a consistent standard of law and custom.

While the doctrine of religion claims that a man is living according to religion if he accepts the caste system and the ideals of the caste to which he belongs. The Karma theory maintains that a man is born into a certain caste because of the outcome of his behavior in the previous incarnation. In the wealthy upper caste, religious confirmation takes place even at birth, and the transgression leads to the creation of lesser and poorer castes.

Because they must go through diksha sanskar, a symbol for rebirth, the first three castes are named Durja (born twice). Shudras, on the other hand, were called Monothetic (once born).

The Shunga dynasty, founded by Pushyamitra Shunga in 184 BC, was the stronghold of "Brahmanism" and led to the strong development of the caste system after the Mauryan period. Despite Manusmuiti, the Brahmins were able to re-establish their dominance and impose strict restrictions on Shudras. Following their journey to India, the Chinese scholars Hiuen Tsang stated that "people who followed unclean occupations such as butchers and manual scavengers had to live outside the city, and Brahmanism was dominant in India." The caste system also governed India's religious life.

7.11 FEATURES OF THE JATI (CASTE SYSTEM) IN INDIA

A society is made up of various small social groups known as castes. All of these races have well-established social groups to which membership is determined by birth. Every caste is further subdivided according to tribe. It is forbidden for people from the same tribe to get married because they are all thought to be descended from the same progenitor.

According to Greek explorer Megasthenes, who lived in India in 300 BC, inherited occupation was one of the two characteristics of the caste system. Although there are limits on food and drink, everyone accepts the meals given by the Brahmins due to their long-standing domination. Although it is identifiable to all races, each has its own name.

Occasionally, a company may be affiliated with a certain caste. By excluding the lower castes and accusing them of tainting their culture, the upper castes preserved their alleged genetic, spiritual, and ceremonial purity. To protect the prestige of each caste, conventions and caste norms go to considerable lengths. The community uses a panchayat, or elected assembly, to carry these out in public.

7.12 MAJOR FUNCTIONS OF THE JATI (CASTE SYSTEM)

Many towns have benefited from its accommodations, which grant each one sole authority over a certain revenue stream. Individuals gained respect in society and social security advantages. A person's caste affects their choice of marriage, as well as the purpose of state clubs, profit groups, and orphanages. By transferring a caste's hereditary skills and knowledge from generation to generation, it has assisted in applying pressure on culture and ensuring productivity. Caste is an important factor in socialization because of its power to transmit cultural norms, values, and customs.

7.13 DISCUSSIONS REGARDING JATI AND VARNA

The Harivamsa informs us that two sons of Nabhagaristha who were Vaisyas became Brahmanas.

Kumarila Bhatla holds that if vrtli or action be the cause of determining one's varna then 'one and the same man would be a Brahmana when performing a good deed, and a Sudra when doing a bed one, and thus there would be no fixity of caste'.

The Munainsaka may hold the fact is that both the jati and the varna theories had been operating in ancient India. Our contention will be clearer in the discussion that follows:

The short account may be sub-divided thus:

(a) An account of equal castes (sajati).
(b) Enumeration of the mixed castes (anulomas, partitions and miscellaneous castes)
(c) Methods bringing change of castes.

"By men of the same varna in domen of the same varna are born sajati, i.e., sons of equal varna. In blameless marriages one (are begotten) continuing the line".

Kautilya and Bodhayana who maintain that sons begotten by one on women of the next lower caste should also be considered to be savarnas.

On the *anantarapurah* Manu observes:

"Some, begotten by twice-born men or wives of the next lower caste, they declare to be similar (to their fathers but) blamed on account of the fault (in hererd) in their mothers.

The pre-Christian age when the *Dharmasutras* and the *Arthasastra* were composed such issues inherited the caste of their fathers, but about 200 A.D. when the *Manu–Samhita* was composed their positions had degraded a little and this degradation became complete during the time of Yajnavalkya.

Yajnavalkya holds that the blameless marriage of the parents was the pre-condition of the birth of a sajala, Vishnu, however, simply states but says nothing about the parents marriage.

The earlier Census Reports show the existence of at least three thousand castes rigidly exclusive in marriage and dining and each claiming superiority over the others. Anthropologists think that this multiplicity is due to the following factors:

(a) The rise of various functional groups that acquired hereditary characters and followed the laws of endogamy and exogamy, e.g., carpenters, potters, goldsmiths, blacksmiths, etc.
(b) The rise of race castes occasioned by entrance of tribal groups in the Brahmnical society.
(c) The emergence of sectarian castes, e.g., the Lingaytas and Vaisnava Castes in Maharashtra, etc.
(d) Other factors, e.g., migration, cross breeding, etc.

Yajnavalkya enumerates six sub-castes murdhavasikts, Ambastha, Nisado, Mahisya Ugra and Karana as anulomas, i.e., born of parents where fathers belong to the higher and the mother to the lower caste or varna. The account runs thus:

(a) "From a Brahmana with the daughters of Ksatriya is born the Musdhavasikta with the daughter of a Vaishya an Ambastha and with the daughter of a Sudra a Nisada or Parasava".

(b) From a Kshatriya man and a Vaisya woman is born a Mahisya, while from a Kshatriya man and a Shudra woman is born an Ugra. Similarly, from a Vaisya man and a Shudra woman is born a Chandala. These terms refer to different social classes or groups in the varna system, reflecting varying degrees of social status and roles.[3]

During the time of the early Dharmasutra writers had gained the status of the Brahmanas but evidently their status was not so high as that of the Brahmanas of the Madhyadesa.

The Nisadas also were an Austro-Asiatic tribe of rude culture and lived outside the Aryandam.

R.P. Chanda points out that in the Pancavimsa Brahmana the performer of the Vivjit sacrifice is required to live for three days among he Nisadas, while in the Srautsutra of Katyayana and in the Mimansastra.

The Dharmasastra writer give them the appellation of Parasava which Manu explains as meaning "a living corpse".

The Mahisyas born from a Ksatriya with the daughter of a Vaisya according to Yajnavalkya, from a very interesting groups. The Brahmanuaivarta Purana states that from such a union is born a Kaivarta.

Manu also refers to six anuloma castes but actually names only three.

(i) Ambasiha
(ii) Nisada
(iii) Ugra

P.V. Kane thinks that when Yajnavalkya states that the aulomas are safe it is meant that they are entitled to samaskaras. According to Yajnavalkya from a Brahmana with the daughter of a Sudra is born a Nisada or Parasava and if he is entitled samaskara then it would show that the anulomas got the status of their further. Kane has pointed out that the Dharmastara writers maintained three different views on the subject. The Ambstha lived in the Western Punjab and are mentioned in the Mahabhartha along with the Sivis and the Yaduheyas.

---

3 Sudhakar Chattopadhyaya, 'Jati and Varna (Caste System) in 'Social Life in Ancient India', Academic Publishers, Calcutta, 1965, pp. 5–25.

The same caste Dr. Raychaudhury points out that "in later times the Ambasthas are found in South-Eastern India near the Mekala range, and also in Bihar and Bengal a Magadha and from a Sudra an Ksatlara, while from a Sudra with a Vaisya girl an Ayogava."

Gautama, Kautilya and Manu give the same account Vaistha names five: Candala, Suta and three new names Antyavasyi, Ramaka and Pukkasa.

The Vaidehakas or the people of Videha and the Magadhas or the people of Magadha are quite well-known tribes playing important parts in the history of ancient India. Janaka, the king of the Vidahans, is treated with respect in the ancient lose.

The Magadha the inhabitants of Patna and Gaya districts of Bihar were not evidently wholly Brahmanised. Pargitas has suggested that it was in their country that the Aryans possibly mingled with a body of invaders who evidently came from the caste by sea."

The Rigveda account of Kikata identified with Magadha, and its chieftain named Pramaganda shows that it was inhabited by an un-Aryan tribe. The Brahmanas, who settled there at a later period, were not held in high as the expression Brahmanandhu Magadhadesiya show:

At the present time they are found in Assam and the Howrah and Midnapur districts of W. Bengal. Some manuscripts of the Vayu Purana state the king Visvaphani or Visvasphaurji who ruled in Magadha just before the rise of the Guptas brought the Kaivartas into prominence.

The Vgras are a tribal caste in Bengal living mainly in the Burdwan and Birbhum districts. Kane paints out that according to the sahyadrikhanda and Sudreekamalakara an Ugra is called Rajput while according to the Pativiveka he is called Raut.

The Angultaranikaya too refers to the close connection of the Ugras with Vesali or Vaisali, the capital of the Vayjian confederation.

Yainavalkya speaks to six sub-castes—Suta, Vaidehaka, Candala, Magadha, Ksattaro and Ayogava—as partitions, i.e., born on parent where father belong to the lower and the mother to the higher caste or varna.

The account runs thus:

"From a Brahmana with the daughters of Ksatriya is born the Murdhavasikta, with the daughters of a Vaisya an Ambastha, and with the daughter of a Sudra a Nisada or Parasava."[4]

"From a Ksatriya with the daughters of a Vaisya and with the daughter of a Sudra are born respectively a Mahisya and an Ugra, while from a Vaisya with the daughter of a sudra is bon a Karana".[5]

---

[4] Sudhakar Chattopadhyaya, 'Jati and Varna (Caste System) in 'Social Life in Ancient India', Academic Publishers, Calcutta, 1965, pp. 5–25.

[5] *Ibid.*

According to Vijananesvara the purpose is that in case that the issue of a mixed caste like Murdhavarikla, Ambartha, Ugra, etc. are married to higher caste and issues of such marriages are likewise married to five or seven consecutive generations then at the sixth or the eighth stage the issues acquire the status of a higher caste.

Yajnavalkya's statement, "by confusion of profession comes equality," is interpreted to mean that when a member of a higher caste adopts the profession of a lower caste, their descendants, after five or seven generations, will belong to the caste or jati associated with that profession.

It is evident that Yajnavalkya describes two different conditions for changing one's caste. We can compare this with the views of earlier Dharmashastra writers, who noted that many of these castes lived outside the Aryavarta regions described by earlier texts.

This Aryavarta is described as follows:

"This region lying to the east of Adarsa or Adarsans (i.e., the place where the river Sarasvati disappears in the sand, the present Hissar in the Punjab); to the west of Kalakauana (usually identified with a wild tract near Prayaga or Allahabad); to the south of the Himalaya, and to the north of the Paripatra (i.e., the western partly of the present Vindhya range) is called Aryavarta".

The countries of Avanti, Anga, Magadha, Surastra, Daksinapatha, Upabhart-Sindhu and Sauvira, i.e., in the belt surrounding it the above Aryavarta. Linguists refer to Aryavarta as the land of the inner band of the Aryan group, while the surrounding regions are known as the outer band of the Aryan group. R.P. Chandra points out that in this outer band, we encounter people of a different stock from the Aryan group of the mid-land. He also notes that these regions are associated with various professions, such as artisans and those engaged in administrative and record-keeping roles. Chandra effectively assigns a large number of these occupational castes to the status of the fourth order.

Manu states:

In consequence of the omission of the sacred rites and of their not consulting Brahmanas, the following tribes of Ksatriyas have gradually sunk in this world to the condition of Sudras. viz., the Paundrakes, the Codes, the Dravidas, the Kambajas, the Yavanas, the Sakes, the Barodas, the Pahlaves, the Cinar, the Kiratas, the Dardoes.

Dr. D.R. Bhandarkar has shown how the Yavanas, Sakas etc. became part and parcel of the Brahmanical society and how they acquired even honourable position. The Great Epic throws much light on this points. Thus speaking of the Sakaduipa, the land of the Sakas eloquent tribute is paid to the tribe and it is started that the four-fold division of the people (caturvarnyan) is also prevalent in the land.

The theory of anuloma and pratiloma was enunciated as they held birth was the basis of social division. In case of the tribal castes, we note a very significant fact. If we analyse the account of the Dharmashastra we find have at its higher stratum a level of Brahmanical culture beneath which were un-Aryan or un-Brahmanical layers.

Yajnavalkya makes the following interesting statement:

"By a (man of the) Mahisya class on a (women of the) Karana class is begotten Rathakara".

The union of a Vaisya male and a Ksatriya female". We need not multiply such examples.

Manu observes:

These races (sub-castes) (which originate) in a confusion (of the castes and) have been described according to their fathers and mothers, may be known by their occupations, whether they conceal or openly show themselves.

Kautilya makes the following interesting observations on this point:

"A vaisya becomes a Rathakara, Chariot-makes, by profession. Member of this castes shall marry among themselves and in customs and avocation they shall follow their ancestors. They may either become Sudras or any other lower caste excepting Candalas. The duty of a Sudra "is the serving of the twice-born (dvijati) in agriculture, and cattle breeding".

Gautama deserves:

"In the seventh (generation men obtain) or change of caste, either being raised to a higher one one being de-graded to a lower one."

Manu states:

"If (a female of the caste) sprung from a Brahmana and a Sudra female bear children to one of the highest caste, the inferior (tribe) attains the highest caste within the seventh generation. Thus a Sudra attains the rank of a Brahmana, and (in a similar manner) a Brahmana sinks to the level of a Sudra, but knows that it is the same with the offspring of a Ksatriya or a Vaisya".

The observation of Yajnavalkya, there is nevertheless a points of difference. Yajnavalkya simply speaks of the rise of the caste evidently through marriage in the fifth or the seventy.

Apastamba on the other hand, maintains that change of caste is only possible in the next birth by means of action of the present one:

"In successive births men of the lower caste are born in the next higher one, if they have fulfilled their duties. In successive births men of the higher castes are born in the next lower one if they neglect their duties."

Gautama and Manu speak of seven births or generations for the change of caste while Yajnavalkya speaks of five or seven. Yjnanesvara gives the following note: In the seventh or fifth and by the use of world 'api' (even) in the text is to be known sixth also". The higher the position of the father and the mother, the gloss shows, the lesser would be the number of generations.

The Baudhayana Dharmasutra makes a very interesting rule:

"In a Nisada (the son of Brahmana from a sudra wife) marries a Nisadi (and this goes on continuously), then the fifth generations becomes free of the taint of a Sudra status; he can have upanayana performed for him and his son (Sixth from the original Nisada pair) can have a vedic sacrifice performed for him".

7.14 CONTROVERSY IN RIGVEDA REGARDING VARNA JATI

The varnas has been known since a hyms in Rigveda (the oldest surviving Indian text) that portrays the Bhraman (Priest) the Kshatriya (nobel), the Vaishya (commoner) and the Shudra (servent) issued fourth at creations from the mouth, arms, thighs and feet of the principal person (parusha). Male of the first three varnas are "twice-born" (divya): after undergoing the ceremony of spiritual rebirth (upanayana), they are initiated into members and all free to study the Vedas. The ancient scriptures of Hinduism. The shudra live in service in turn as common people, grazers, and cultivate contrast with the governing classes, i.e., the secular Kshatriya or Barons and the sacerdotal Brahmanas. Brahmans and Kshatriya themselves contrast in that the former are the priests, while the latter have the actual domination. In the older description far greater emphasis is placed on the functions of the classes than on hereditary membership, in contradistinctions to caste which emphasis heredity over functions.

The system of the four classes (caturvarnya) is fundamental to the views the traditional lawgivers held of society. They specified a different set of obligations for each. The task of the Brahman is to study and advise the baron to protect the Vaishya to cultivate and the Sudra to serve.

History shows, however, that the four-class system was mere a social model, then a reality. the multitudinous of castes (or jati) is explained as the result of hypergamous and hypogamous alliance between the four classes and their descendants.

The inclusion of the shudra on them a measure of dignity. A move to accommodate still other not so distinguished to the rather unofficial acceptance of a fifth class. The Pancama (Sanskrit : "fifth"), which include the "untouchable" classes and others, such as tribal groups, who are outside the system and, consequently, avarna ("classes"). In modern times, traditional Hindus, awakened to the inequities of the caste system yet believing the four-varna system to be fundamental to the good society, have often advocated a return to this clear-cut varna system by reframing castes. Individual castes, in turn, have sought to raise their social rank by identifying with a particular varna and demanding its privileges of rank and honour.

CITPAVAN

Citpavan also called ponkanosth caste of Brahmans live in poran (the area of Goa) and Maharashtra state in western India. They rose to considerable eminence in Maharastra as administrators during the rule of the Peshwas of Poona (1713-1818) who belonged to the caste. The predominance among them of fair complexions and light-coloured eyes has given rise to the speculation that they are descended from shipwrecked European sailors, while many Citpavan Brahmanas continue the administrative tradition, others are active in other professions.

CETTI

Cetti group of castes widespread in southern India, roughly corresponding to the Banias, a similar group of merchant castes in the north. They specialize primarily in the mercantile treades, as bankers, moneylenders, pawn-brokers, shopkeepers and merchants. They employ a special trade jargaon which contain more or less secret name for figures among certain cetti castes. Mass weddings were held at intervals of 10 or 15 years, apparently for reasons of economy such as marriage season would last for many months[6].

Jati

Jati also spelled jati caste in Hindu society. The term is derived from the Sanskrit jata, "born" or "brought into existence" and indicates a form of existence determined by birth. In Indian Philosophy jati (genus) describes any group of things that have generic characteristics in common sociologically. Jati has come to be used universally to indicate a caste group among Hindus.

The earliest Vedic text listed the Kshatriya (holders of kshatra, or authority) as first in rank then the Brahmans (Priests and teachers of law), next the Vaishya (merchant-traders), and finally the Shudra (artisans and labourers). Movement of individuals and groups from one class to another both upward and downward, were not uncommon; a rise in status was a recognized reward for outstanding service to the rulers of the day.

Maithil

Maithil Brahman caste of Brahmans in Bihar India (the area of the ancient kingdom of Mithila) well known for their orthodoxy and interesting in learning. Maithil Brahman has a distinct culture, tradtions, art-forms, like Madhubani-Paintings, dialects, language, etc. Mithil Brahmins are

---

[6] P. Sharan, *Ancient Indian Political Thought and Institutions,* Meenakshi Prakashan, Merrut, 1978.

the Hindu Brahmin community originating from the Mithila region of the Indian subcontinent that comprises Tirhut, Dharbhanga, Kosi, Purnia, Munger, Bhagalpur and Santhal pargana divisions of India.

Kshatriya

Kshatriya also spelled kastriya, second highest in rituals status of the four varnas or social classes of Hindu in India, traditionally the military or ruling class.

Kshatriya were destroyed by Parasurama the sixth avatar of Vishnu ji as a punishment for their tyranny is thought by some scholars to reflect a long struggle for supremacy between priest and rulers. Brahmanic texts such as the Manusmriti (a book of Hindu law) and most other dharmashastras (work of jurisprudence) report a Brahman victory, but epic texts often after a different account, and it is likely that in social reality rulers have usually ramped first. The persistent representation of dalits (especially Vishnuji, Krishna ji and lord Ramaji) as rulers underscores the point, as does the elaborate services of rutiual roles and privileges pertaining history, through most of Hindus history. These largely buttress the image of a ruler as preserver of dharma (religious and moral law) and auspicious wealth. In modern times the Kshatriya varna includes a board class of caste groups, differing considerably in status and function but united by their claims to rulership, the pursuit of war or the possession of the land.

7.15 GEOGRAPHICAL EXPANSION OF TRIBES IN ANCIENT INDIA

The Rigveda is the only source to give us an idea of the geographical expanse of the Early Vedic period. When the early Rigvedic hymns were written, the focus of Aryan culture was the margin between the Jamuna and Sutudri (Sutlej) and along the upper course of the river Saraswati.

The geographical area eventually occupied by the Rigvedic tribes is clearly indicated by the mention of river and mountains localities, tribes and kingdoms which permit of easy identification. The Rigveda mentions the following rivers: Kubha (modern Kabul), the Suvastu (Swal), the Krumu (Kurram), the Gomati (Gumal), the Sindhu (Indus) and its tributaries, viz. Vistasta (Jhelum), Askin (Chenab), Parushri (Ravi), Studri (Sutlej), and Vipasa (Beas), the Soshma (Sohan), the Marudrividha (Maryaunardica), the Saraswati the Drishadvati (the Rapshi or Chitang), the Yamuna, the Ganga and the Saraua.

The mention of these rivers implies the possession by the Aryans of a considerable portion of the country stretching from earlier Afghanistan to the upper valley of Ganges. The major part of this area came to be known as Sapta Sindhu or the land of the seven rivers by the Aryans (comprising the five tributaries of the river Indus and the Sarasvati). The country of the

Aryans was also designated as Aryavarta in the latter scriptures.[7]

The Rigvedic Aryans were not acquainted with the seas or oceans. Rigveda mentions the word Samudra which probably means only a collection of water and not sea in this period. The Rigvedic Aryans were not familier with any kind of desert.

The Himalaya or the Himavanta mountains are well known to the Rigvedic sage but not the Vindhyas or Satpuras. Other hills referred to include the Aryika Meyavant, identified as the source of Soma, and the Suleman Ridge, among others.

The entire territory known to the Vedic Aryans was divided into several tribal principalities, typically ruled by the leaders of the tribes or kings. In the Dasarajna Yuddha (the Battle of Ten Kings), described in various Rigvedic hymns, many important Vedic tribes and their leaders are mentioned.

The battle was between Sudas a Bharata king of the Tribes family and the tribal confederacy of then kings led by Visnumitra; the federation consisting of the five well-known tribes Puru, Yadu, Turvasa, Anu and Drecheya—Allong with five of little note, viz. Alina, Paptha, Bhabnas, Siva and Vishanin.

In the bloody struggle at the banks of river Parushni (Ravi), the Bharatas emerged victorious. The Sudas had to fight against the three non-Aryan tribes—Ajas, Sigrees and Yakshus under the leadership of king Bheda, but these new association were also defeated on the banks of river Yamuna.

The Bharatas were in the Rigvedic age settled in the region between the Saraswati and Yamuna. The Purus were another very important tribe living on either side of the Saraswati. The Anus, Pythyes, Yadus and Turvasas were the allies of the Purus against the Bharatas.

These five are the Panchjanah (the five people) of the Rigveda according to Zimer, Yadu and Turvasa tribes lived in the southern Punjab. The extreme north-west was occupied by the Gandharis, Pakthas, Alinas, Bhouanas and Vishanins. Chedi was an ancient Indian mahajanapada, a kingdom which fell roughly in the Bundelkhand division of Madhya Pradesh regions to the south of river Yamuna along the river Ken. Its capital city was called Suktimati in Sanskrit and Sotthivati-nagara in Pali. The chief opponents of the Aryans were the indigenous people of non-Aryans origin such as Panis and Dasas. The Panis in Rigveda are described as wealthy people who refused to patronize the Vedic preists and perform Vedic rituals, and who stole the cattle of the Aryans. More hated than the Panis were the Dasas or Dasyees who were black-skinned malignant and non-sacrificing and spoke a language totally different from that of the Aryans. Others prominent Non-Aryan Tribes were the Amasa Ayagna, Avrata, Akasman, Asura, Murdvork, etc.

---

[7] Beni Prasad, *The state in Ancient India*, Prayagraj, The Indian Press limited, 1928.

Later Vedic Period (1000–600 B.C.)

The period was marked by further expansions of the Aryans to part of eastern Uttar Pradesh, northern Bihar and parts of eastern Rajasthan. The Sathaptha Brahmana throws light on this expansion to the eastern Gangetic Plains.

It reports the founding of a realm called 'Vidha' by a Prince Videgha Madhava. The Purus and the Bhartas were amalgamated to form the Kurus the kingdom of which corresponding to modern Thaneswar Delhi and the upper Gangetic Doab. The Panchalas were also a composite class whose territory roughly corresponds to the modern day Bareilly, Badaun, Farrukhabad and adjoining districts. The major socio-political centre of this period was the puru-Panchal janapada of the Ganga-Yamuna doab.

Further, regions to the east, such as Kosala (eastern Uttar Pradesh, its early capital was Ayodhya, later replaced by Saraswati, Kashi (Varanasi), Videha (north Bihar), Magadha (South Bihar), Anga (set up their settlements on the rivers Son and the Ganges) and Vangas (eastern Bengal). Northern tribes were the Uttarakurus, the Uttara Madras, Gandhari, Kambojas and the Kekayas. In south India there were tribes like Satvantas, Vidarbhas, Nishadas, etc. Some non-Aryans tribes of the later vedic period mentioned in the Aitareya Brahmana are the Andhra Pandras Sataras, Pulindas matribs.

The later Vedic texts mentions rivers such as the Narmada, Gandak, Chambal, etc. The Satapatha Brahmana mentions the eastern and western Seas (Bay of Bengal and Arabian Sea). The later three Vedas give three broad divisions of India, viz. Aryavarta (Northern India), Madhagadesa (Central India), and Dakshinpatha (Souther India).[8]

Caste is a system that has been a part of Indian society since ancient times, according to its structural makeup. The caste system is accepted by society despite varying opinions regarding its origins. Indian culture, customs, caste, and creeds are still very much in effect today. Practically speaking, the caste system's idea of high and low stratification is expressed. Caste and caste-based traditions exist in society, however discrimination on the basis of caste is prohibited under the constitution. Regarding Indian society, which dates back to the Vedic era, varna and caste can be considered as a means of understanding. Nonetheless, the varna system was not entirely disappearing. But the varna system was far from extinct. It has been demonstrated by Dr. D.R. Bhandarkar how different alien tribes that came to India in the past were accepted into the caste system.

7.16 NICHOLAS DIRKS VIEW ON CASTE

In his 2001 book "Castes of Mind: Colonialism and the Making of Modern India," American scholar Nicholas B. Dirks (1947) described how the Indian

---

[8] Beni Prasad, *The state in Ancient India*, Prayagraj, The Indian Press limited, 1928.

caste system was supported by the census and the power of the colonial masters to govern. In reality, according to Nicholas Dirks, caste is neither a monolithic system that embodies a fundamental cultural ideal nor an unaltered holdover from ancient India. Caste is a recent phenomenon that emerged from a specific historical encounter between India and British colonial control, rather than being a fundamental representation of Indian tradition. Dirks does not claim that the British invented caste. However, caste did unify into a single term under British rule, one that could encompass India's many social identities and organizational structures. From the commentaries of an eighteenth-century Jesuit to the enumerative obsessions of the late nineteenth-century census, Dirks traces the career of caste from the medieval kingdoms of southern India to the textual traces of early colonial archives; from the ethnographic writings of colonial administrators to those of twentieth-century Indian scholars seeking to rescue ethnography from its colonial legacy. In addition, his book examines the development of caste politics in the 20th century, paying particular attention to the advent of caste-based movements that have put the consensus of nationalists in jeopardy[9].

7.17 VARNA AND JATI ACCORDING TO DIPANKAR GUPTA

Renowned sociologist Dipankar Gupta offers perceptive viewpoints on the ideas of Varna and Jati in Indian society. For ages, the social structure of India has been molded by two significant social constructs: Varna and Jati. Varna is the name given to the four divisions of society found in the Rigveda and other ancient Indian literature. The four Varnas are Shudras (workers and servants), Vaishyas (merchants and farmers), Kshatriyas (warriors and rulers), and Brahmins (priests and scholars).Varna, in Gupta's view, is a theoretical construct that symbolizes an idealized social structure predicated on social positions and employment. According to Gupta, Varna is a framework that is flexible enough to allow for social mobility rather than a rigid system. He underlines that individuals can travel across Varnas based on their abilities and achievements. Gupta does concede, though, that social mobility has really been restricted and that Varna has frequently been connected to social position and inherited profession.[10]

According to Deepakar Gupta, "The Indian caste system: From the Asiatic to the feudal mode of production" (from Varna to Jati), the two main modes of production in Asia were Varna and Jati. Varna was characterized by general exploitation, while Jati was the result of feudal

[9] Nicholas B. Dirks, *Castes of Mind: Colonialism and the Making of Modern India*, Princeton, NJ: Princeton University Press, 2001, pp. 63–80.

[10] Dipankar Gupta, "From Varna to to Jati: The Indian Caste system: from Asiatic to the Feudal Mode of Production", *Journal of Contemporary Asia*, Vol. 10: 3, 2008, pp. 249–271.

mode production, which was characterized by localized exploitation in a closed village. Jati's agricultural operations were open to all categories of the Varna scheme, and the lower orders were quite self-sufficient, making it difficult to distinguish between peasants and artisans.

The various castes or subgroups that are present within each Varna are referred to as jati. On the other hand, Jati is mostly determined by birth and is defined by endogamy, or intracaste marriage, and professional specialization. In contrast to Varna, Gupta contends that Jati is a more tangible and confined social unit. An individual's occupation, social contacts, and social identity are determined by Jati.

Gupta emphasizes that Jati is a multifaceted social phenomena that includes a range of elements like social hierarchy, kinship, occupation, and rituals. Every Jati has its own set of traditions, practices, and regulations that control how its members behave and relate to one other. In a community, jati is essential for preserving social harmony and controlling interpersonal interactions. Gupta highlights the relationship yet distinction between the ideas of Varna and Jati. Jati is the actual expression of social division, whereas Varna is the theoretical underpinning.

Gupta contends that the link between Varna and Jati is dynamic and multifaceted, providing a broad classification of society into four primary categories, while Jati further subdivides these categories into innumerable unique groups. Varna offers a broad framework, while Jati gives each Varna additional layers of variation and specificity. According to Gupta, Jati has frequently been employed as a tool for social exclusion and control, which has resulted in the continuation of prejudice and inequality.[11]

Gupta clarifies the intricate workings of the Indian social order through his examination of Varna and Jati. He highlights the possibility of social mobility and refutes the idea that Varna is a fixed and unyielding structure. Gupta also emphasizes how Jati controls social relationships and shapes social identities. Gupta's viewpoint has, nevertheless, not been without criticism. Some contend that by emphasizing social mobility, he ignores the discrimination and institutional obstacles that prevent excluded groups from moving up the social mobility ladder. Some argue that Gupta's argument falls short in addressing how caste intersects with other types of social inequalities including class and gender.

Dipankar Gupta's comprehension of Varna and Jati offers important insights into the Indian social order. His approach emphasizes the intricate and nuanced nature of caste-based social boundaries while highlighting the dynamic link between Varna and Jati. Even if Gupta's point of view has had a significant impact, it is crucial to take into account opposing arguments and current discussions about these ideas.[12]

---

[11] Dipankar Gupta, "From Varna to to Jati: The Indian Caste system: from Asiatic to the Feudal Mode of Production", *Journal of Contemporary Asia*, Vol. 10: 3, 2008, pp. 249–271.

[12] *Ibid.* pp. 249–271.

Ideally, the capitalist system creates a new differentiation hierarchy based on capital's exploitation of labor. However, civilizations that display a single mode of production to the complete exclusion of other modes—that is, in its "pure" form—rarely exist. In a civilization, as in India, many modes of production can and do coexist, with "one being dominant, i.e., governing the basic relations of the society". Thus, it would be asking too much for a casteless society in contemporary India, where pre-capitalist elements still predominate and capitalism was introduced without the accompanying industrial revolution (socialist or capitalist). Meillassoux has convincingly shown that capitalists in developing nations take use of these pre-capitalist systems for "super exploitation" since they would rather not take on "the functions of social security". Because of the uncertainty of capitalist exploitation, the traditional links to the hamlet, clan, caste, and feudal lord were therefore strengthened rather than broken.

During the feudal era, a small number of landowners held the majority of the land, which served as both a socio-political authority base and an indicator of wealth. More vocational specialization resulted from this, as well as the need to develop social norms and economic exchanges between the middle and lower orders. Ultimately, a closer look at the origins of the varna system—the conquest by Aryans who enslaved the native populations—will help us comprehend the strict endogamy restrictions and the "natural superiority" justification that drive the]atis. There was a clear racial divide between these two groups, which offered an easy justification for the indigenous tribes' subjugation—specifically, the metaphor of color. The idea of "natural superiority" and the rites that sanctified it were deeply ingrained in Indian society for this reason alone; the relevance of this myth is often overlooked. We have tried to connect varna and]ati to the mode of production in order to understand the history and peculiarities of the caste system in India. We also find that understanding the varna system in general and the rigidity and ritualism of the]ati in particular requires an understanding of the ideological framework of the system in relation to the unique characteristics of the socio-economic formations of its time period. Therefore, we reject Srinivas' argument that the caste system makes sense in its omission of the varna model. According to Srinivas, the untouchables are not allowed in the varna system even though "they are an integral part of the society."

It is crucial to discuss the unique contextual circumstances of India, which gave rise to distinct economic formations that served as the foundation for the caste system and varna/jati under the various economic eras typically referred to as the Asiatic and feudal modes of production. This strategy will lessen the prejudice against the Eurocentric attempts to condemn Indian society to a state of eternal stagnation and timelessness. Ultimately, the study is expected to spark a reconsideration of the Asian method of production and its dominance of the social structure during a pivotal period in Indian history[13].

MODEL QUESTIONS FOR PRACTICE

7.1 Discuss the meaning, connotations and features of Varna and Jati in Indian political thoughts.

7.2 Varna gave a theoretical framework to the Jati which was the real and practical basis of the Indian Social system; In the light of the statement discuss the role of Varna and Jati in Indian Social system.

7.3 Use of Caste for both Varna and Jati has confounded (confused) the different origin and role of Varna and Jati in Indian Social system.

7.4 Despite an egalitarian constitution, the caste is still a reality of Indian social system; do you agree? Give arguments in support of your views.

---

[13] *Ibid.*

Glossary

Daṇḍa (an ancient symbol of authority) is the Hindu term for punishment. In ancient India, punishments were generally sanctioned by the ruler. Daṇḍa provides a way for an offender to right any violations of dharma that he or she may have committed.

Dharma is the moral value of the Individual. It is associated with moral code of conduct or may be a set of dutiesof the king and religious convictions of the human beings. Dharma signifies the eternal laws which maintain the world.

Dharmaśāstra (Sanskrit: धर्मशास्त्र) is a genre of Sanskrit texts on law and conduct, and refers to the treatises (śāstras) on dharma. Unlike Dharmasūtra which are based upon Vedas, these texts are mainly based on Puranas. There are many Dharmashastras, variously estimated to be 18 to about 100, with different and conflicting points of view. Each of these texts exist in many different versions, and each is rooted in Dharmasutra texts dated to 1st millennium BCE that emerged from Kalpa (Vedanga) studies in the Vedic era.

Manu-saṁhitā, which is the law of the human race. Manusmṛti also known as Mānava-Dharmaśāstra is the most important and earliest metrical work of the Dharmaśāstra textual tradition of Vedic society.

Matsya-Nyaya is an ancient Indian philosophy which refers to the principle of the *Law of Fish*. It is described as the fundamental law of nature explained by the proverb of the big fish devouring the smaller fish, hence strong devour the weak. It can be equated to the 'Law of the Jungle'. In simple words, The strong dominates over the weak when there is disorder. Ancient Indian political thought as given in the niti (moral law) lays down that matsya nyaya (big fish swallowing the smaller fish), which is a law of nature, must be eradicated.

Mīmāṁsā is a Sanskrit word that means "reflection" or "critical investigation" and thus refers to a tradition of contemplation which reflected on the meanings of certain Vedic texts. This tradition is also known as Pūrva-Mīmāṁsā because of its focus on the earlier (*pūrva*) Vedic texts dealing with ritual actions, and similarly as Karma-Mīmāṁsā due to its focus on ritual action (*karma*). It is one of six Vedic "affirming" (āstika) schools of Hinduism.

Moksha literally means freedom from samsara. This concept of liberation or release is shared by a wide spectrum of religious traditions, including Hinduism, Buddhism, and Jainism. Moksha, also spelled mokṣa, also called mukti, in Indian philosophy and religion, liberation from the cycle of death and rebirth (*samsara*).

Nikaya is a Pali word meaning "volume" to mean "collection", "assemblage", "class" or "group" in both Pali and Sanskrit. It is most commonly used in reference to the Pali Buddhist texts of the Tripitaka namely those found in the Sutta Pitaka.

Prāyaścitta is the Sanskrit word which means "atonement, penance, expiation". In Hinduism, it is a *dharma*-related term and refers to voluntarily accepting one's errors and misdeeds, confession, repentance, means of penance and expiation to undo or reduce the karmic consequences. It includes atonement for intentional and unintentional misdeeds. The ancient Hindu literature on repentance, expiation and atonement is extensive, with earliest mentions found in the Vedic literature.

Purusha suktam (Sanskrit पुरुषसूक्तम्) is hymn of the Rigveda, dedicated to the Purusha, the "Cosmic Being". It is also found in the Shukla Yajurveda Samhita and Atharvaveda Samhita.

Rectitude refers to behavior that is morally correct behavior or thinking, righteousness, upright and honorable.

Shukranīti is a part of Dharmasastra and considered as *Shukracharya's System of Morals*. It is a treatise on the science of governance, structured towards upholding the morals through implementing theories of political science. Shukraniti focuses on morality, which it stresses is necessary for the overall well being of the people and the state (Rajya). Thus, attempts to regulate the economic, social, and political aspects of human activity.

The Aitareya Brahmana is the Brahmana of the Shakala Shakha of the Rigveda, an ancient Indian collection of sacred hymns. The First Chapter of the Aitareya Upanishad explains the creation of the world. It states that all living beings emerge from the self and desire to have company. It also states that Brahman created the cosmic being, Purusha, by first creating the organs and then, he created the body. The Aitareya Brahmana is the Brahmana of the Shakala Shakha of the Rigveda, an ancient Indian collection of sacred hymns. This work, according to the tradition, is ascribed to Mahidasa Aitareya.

The Avesta is the primary collection of religious texts of Zoroastrianism, composed in the Avestan language. The Avesta texts fall into several different categories, arranged either by dialect, or by usage. The principal text in the liturgical group is the *Yasna*, which takes its name from the Yasna ceremony, Zoroastrianism's primary act of worship, and at which the *Yasna* text is recited.

The Brahma Purana is one of the eighteen major Puranas collections of Hindu texts in Sanskrit Language. It is listed as the first Maha-Purana in all the anthologies, and therefore also called Adi Purana. Another title for this text is Saura Purana, because it includes many chapters related to Surya or the Sun God. The Brahma Purana is actually just a compilation of geographical Mahatmya (Travel Guides) and sections on diverse topics.

The Dharmashastra literature, written in Sanskrit, exceeds 5,000 titles. It can be divided into three categories: (1) sutras (terse maxims), (2) *smriti*s (shorter or longer treatises in stanzas), and (3) *nibandha*s (digests of *smriti* verses from various quarters) and *vritti*s (commentaries upon individual continuous *smriti*s). The *nibandha*s and *vritti*s, juridical works intended for legal advisers, exhibit considerable skill in harmonizing divergent sutras and *smriti*s.

The Nitisara of Kamandaka, also known as the Kamandakiya-Nitisara, was composed during the period of Gupta Dynasty. It was based on Kautilya's Arthashastra. Nitisara (transl. Essence of Statesmanship) or the Nitisara of Kamandaki, is an ancient Indian treatise on politics and statecraft. It was authored by Kamandaka, also known as Kamandaki or Kamandakiya, who was a disciple of Chanakya. It contains 19 sections. The work has been dedicated to Chandragupta of Pataliputra. Scholars presume that the work was modelled after the Hitopadesha. The *Kāmandakīya Nītisāra* is considered to be a post-Mauryan treatise for it refers to the Mauryan emperor Chandragupta by name. Nitisara contains 20 sargas (chapters) and 36 prakarans. It is based on the Arthasastra of Kautilya and deals with various social elements such as theories of social order, structure of the state, obligations of the ruler, governmental organization, principles and policies of the government, interstate relationships, ethics of envoys and spies, application of different political expedients, varieties of battle arrays, attitude towards morality, and so forth.

Bibliography

A.S. Altekar, "Origin and Types of the State" in State and Government in Ancient India, Motilal Banarsidass, Banaras, 1949, pp. 12–23.

Aiyanagar, K.V.R., (1932), Aspects of the Hindu View of Life: According to the Dharmasastra, Baroda.

Amartya Sen, "Introduction" in The Idea of Justice, Harvard University Press, 2009 Sarkar, Benoy Kumar Political Institutions, and theories of comparative Politics, pp. 158–162.

Annie Besant, *Dharma,* Theosophical Publishing House, Madras, 1964, p. 1.

Anthony D. Smith, *National Identity*, Penguin, London, 1991, p. 43.

Ashutosh Dayal Mathur, *Medieval Hindu Law: Historical Evolution and Enlightened Rebellion,* Oxford University Press, 2007.

Benedict Anderson, *Imagined Community*, Verso, New York, 1983, p. 55.

Beni Prasad, The State in Ancient India: Study in the Structure and Practical Working of Political Institutions in North India in Ancient Times, The Indian Press, Allahabad, 1928, pp. 1–16.

Benoy Kumar Sarkar, "The Hindu Theory of the State", *Political Science Quarterly*, Vol. 36, No. 1 (March 1921), pp. 79–90.

Bhardwaj, H.C. (1979), Aspects of Ancient Indian Technology, Delhi.

C.E. Bosworth, "An Early Arabic Mirror for Princes: Ṭāhir Dhū l-Yamīnain's Epistle to His Son Abdallāh (206/821)," *Journal of Near Eastern Studies,* Jan., 1970, Vol. 29, No. 1 (Jan., 1970), pp. 25–41.

Chakladar, H.C. (1929), Social life in Ancient India: Studies in Vatsysyana are Kamasutra, Calcutta.

Charles Tilly, 'Reflections on the History of European state-making' in Tilly, C. (ed.), *The formation of National States in Europe*, Princeton University Press, Princeton, 1975, p. 42.

Clifford Angell Bates, "The Trajectory of Machiavelli's Concept of State in Early Modern Politics," *Dialogi Polityczne*, November, 2022, 1(32), pp. 9–10.

Clifford Angell Bates, "The Trajectory of Machiavelli's Concept of State in Early Modern Politics," *Dialogi Polityczne*, November, 2022, 1(32), p. 7.

Dipankar Gupta, "From Varna to Jati: The Indian Caste System, from the Asiatic to the Feudal Mode of Production", *Journal of Contemporary Asia*, Vol. 10: 3, 2008. pp. 249–271.

Donald R. Davis Jr, "*Rectitude and Rehabilitation (danda) in the Spirit of Hindu Law*, Cambridge University Press, N.Y., 2010, pp. 128–143.

Gavin Flood, *An Introduction to Hinduism*, Cambridge University Press, Cambridge, 1996, p. 56.

George H. Sabine, "The Concept of the State as Power," *The Philosophical Review* , July 1920, Vol. 29, No. 4 (July 1920), p. 302.

Ghoshal U.N., A History of Hindu Political theory OUP: London, 1983, pp. 213–222, 247–259.

H.N. Sinha, 1938, Sovereignty in Ancient Indian Polity, London, Luzacc and Company.

Hermann Kulke, (ed.), *The State in India 1000–1700*, OUP, Delhi, 1995.

J. Crawford, *The Creation of States in International Law*, 2nd edition, Claredon Press, 2006, p. 4.

J.D.B. Miller, *A World of States*, Croom Helm, London, 1981.

J. Duncan Derrett, "Two Inscriptions Concerning the Status of Kammalas and the Application of Dharmaśāstra" in *Essays in Classical and Modern Hindu Law*, Vol. 1, Leiden E.J. Brill, 1976.

Jagadish P. Sharma, "Non-Monarchical Governments in Vedic India" Republics in Ancient India. Brill, Leiden, 1968, pp. 15–60.

James L. Fitzgerald, "*Dharma* and its Translation in the *Mahābhārata*" in Patrick Olivelle (ed.), *Dharma: Studies in its Semantic, Cultural and Religious History*, Motilal Banarsidass Publishers Private Limited, Delhi, 2009.

Joel P. Brereton, "*Dharman* in the *Ṛgveda*", in Patrick Olivelle (ed.), *Dharma: Studies in its Semantic, Cultural and Religious History*, Motilal Banarsidass Publishers Private Limited, Delhi, 2009.

John Brockington, "The Concept of *Dharma* in the *Rāmāyaṇa*" in Patrick Olivelle (ed.), *Dharma: Studies in its Semantic, Cultural and Religious History*, Motilal Banarsidass Publishers Private Limited, Delhi, 2009.

John Dunn, *The Cunning of Unreason*, Harper Collins, New York, 2000, p. 66.

John E. Tashjean, "On Theory of Statecraft," *The Review of Politics* , July 1973, Vol. 35, No. 3 (July 1973), p. 379.

John E. Tashjean, "On Theory of Statecraft," *The Review of Politics* , July 1973, Vol. 35, No. 3 (July 1973), p. 378.

John Ross Carter, Traditional Definitions of the Term "Dhamma" Philosophy East and West, Vol. 26, No. 3 (July 1976), pp. 329–337.

Joseph Strayer, *Feudalism*, Van Nostrand, Princeton, 1965, p. 30.

K.P. Jayaswal (1924), Hindu Polity, Calcutta.

K.P. Jayaswal (1955), Hind Polity, Bangalore Printing and Publishing Company Limited.

Louise Marlow (ed.), Medieval Muslim Mirrors for Princes: An Anthology of Arabic, Persian and Turkish Political Advice, Cambridge University Press, 2023.

Margaret Chatterjee, "The Concept of Dharma" in M.C. Doeser and J.N. Kraay (eds.) Facts and Values, Philosophical reflections from Western and Non-Western Perspectives, Martinus Nijhoff Publishers, Dordrecht, 1986, pp. 177–188.

Nicholas B. Dirks, Castes of Mind: Colonialism and the Making of Modern India, Princeton, NJ: Princeton University Press, 2001, pp. 63–80.

Olle Qvarnstrom, "*Dharma* in Jainism—A Preliminary Survey" in Patrick Olivelle (ed.), *Dharma: Studies in its Semantic, Cultural and Religious History*, Motilal Banarsidass Publishers Private Limited, Delhi, 2009.

Partha Chatterjee, "All Nations are Modern" in The Truths and Lies of Nationalisms: As narrated by Charvak, Permanent Black, 2021. pp. 5–25.

Patrick Olivelle (ed.), *Dharma: Studies in its Semantic, Cultural and Religious History*, Motilal Banarsidass Publishers Private Limited, Delhi, 2009.

Patrick Olivelle (ed.), *Dharma: Studies in its Semantic, Cultural and Religious History*, Motilal Banarsidass Publishers Private Limited, Delhi, 2009, p. 85.

Patrick Olivelle (tr.), *Manu's Code of Law: A Critical Edition and Translation of the Mānava Dharmaśāstra,* Oxford University Press, New Delhi, 2004.

Patrick Olivelle, "Dharmaśāstra: A Textual History", in Timothy Lubin, Donald R. Davis Jr. and Jayanth K. Krishnan (ed.), *Hinduism and Law: An Introduction*, Cambridge University Press, U.K., 2010, p. 31.

Patrick Olivelle, "Semantic History of *Dharma*: Middle and Late Vedic Periods", in Patrick Olivelle (ed.), *Dharma: Studies in its Semantic, Cultural and Religious History,* Motilal Banarsidass Publishers Private Limited, Delhi, 2009.

Paul Horsch, "From Creation Myth to World Law" in Patrick Olivelle (ed.), *Dharma: Studies in its Semantic, Cultural and Religious History*, Motilal Banarsidass Publishers Private Limited, Delhi, 2009.

Prasad, Beni (1927), Theory of Government in Ancient India (post-Vedic), Abhijeet publications, New Delhi Jayaswal, K.P. (2013), Hindu Polity, Vishvabharti Publications, New Delhi.

Quentin Skinner, 'The State' in Ball, T., Farr, J. and Hanson, R. (eds.), Political innovation and conceptual change: Cambridge University Press, Cambridge, 1989, p. 326.

R.K. Mukherji (1992), Local self-government in Ancient India, Oxford.

R.S. Sharma, "Sabha and Samiti" in *Aspects of Political Ideas and Institutions in Ancient India*, Motilal Banarsidass Publishers, Delhi 1999, reprint. pp. 105–118.

Radha Krishna Choudhry, "Theory of Punishment in Ancient India", in Proceedings of the Indian History Congress, Vol. 10, 1947, pp. 166–171.

René Grotenhuis, *Nation-Building as Necessary Effort in Fragile States*, Amsterdam University Press, 2016, p. 33.

René Grotenhuis, *Nation-Building as Necessary Effort in Fragile States*, Amsterdam University Press, 2016, p. 28.

Richard Devetak, The Modern State, in Richard Devetak, Anthony Burke, Jim George (eds.), *An Introduction to International Relations*, Cambridge University Press, Cambridge, p. 138.

Richard W. Lariviere, "Dharmaśāstra, Custom, 'Real Law' and 'Apocryphal' *Smṛtis*", in Patrick Olivelle (ed.), *Dharma: Studies in its Semantic, Cultural and Religious History*, Motilal Banarsidass Publishers Private Limited, Delhi, 2009.

Robert Lingat, *The Classical Law of India*, Munshiram Manoharlal Publishers Pvt. Ltd., 1993.

Robin Waterfield, *Plato of Athens: A Life in Philosophy*, Oxford University Press, New York, 2023.

Rupert Gethin, "He who sees Dhamma sees Dhammas: Dhamma in Early Buddhism" in *Journal of Indian Philosophy*, Vol. 32, No. 5/6 (December 2004), pp. 513–542.

Rupert Gethin titled "He Who Sees *Dhamma* Sees *Dhammas*: *Dhamma* in Early Buddhism" in Patrick Olivelle (ed.), *Dharma: Studies in its Semantic, Cultural and Religious History*, Motilal Banarsidass Publishers Private Limited, Delhi, 2009.

Saletore, Bhasker Anand (1963), Ancient Indian Political Thought and Institutions, Asia Publishing House, Bombay.

Sharma, R.S. (2005), Aspects of Political Ideas and Institutions in Ancient India, Motilal Banarsidass, New Delhi.

Sudhakar Chattopadhyaya, "Jati and Varna (Caste System)", in *Social Life in Ancient India*, Academic Publishers, Calcutta, 1965, pp. 7–29.

Sushma Yadav and Ram Avtaran Sharma (2000), Indian State: Origin and Development, AAkaar Publications, Delhi.

U.N. Ghosal (1923), *A History of Indian Political Theories*, Calcutta.

Vedprakash Arya and Manohar G. Metre, *Ancient Indian Political Ideas and Institutions*, Current Publications, 2003.

Wendy Doniger and Brian K. Smith (tr.), *The Laws of Manu*, Penguin Books, 1990.

Werner Menski, *Hindu Law: Beyond Tradition and Modernity*, Oxford University Press, New Delhi, 2003.

Index

Ideas and Institutions in Indian Political Thought

Shubhra Parmar • Tanni Moitra

Based on the NEP syllabus, the book serves as a comprehensive introduction to the foundation of ancient Indian political thought from a historical perspective. It aims to offer insights into the diverse theories, principles, and philosophies that structured ancient Indian society. By focusing on institutional history, the text delves into various components of the state as an institution, illustrating how these encompassed not only political but also social, economic, religious, and ethical dimensions of governance and statecraft.

The book offers perspectives on the history and structure of the state in ancient India, discussing political concepts, organizations, types, architecture, and governance. It explores the norms, duties, and responsibilities that governed the state and its institutions, highlighting conceptual changes from various scholarly interpretations of ancient texts.

Drawing upon ancient and medieval literature, the book addresses key concepts of Indian political consciousness, including dharma (dhamma), danda, niti, nyaya, sabha, samiti, rajya, rashtra, varna, and jati. It acquaints students with these concepts, serving as theoretical and conceptual pillars for understanding ancient Indian social and political ideas. Besides, it enlightens students about the concepts of Dharma and Danda, and the methods used in ancient India's Nyaya (justice), Niti (ethics/policy), Sabha (assembly), and Samiti (committee) practices. It also covers the development of Rajya (kingdom) and Rashtra (nation) and explains Varna's workings and its distinction from caste (jati).

The book primarily caters to the needs of B.A. Political Science students. The students of Philosophy and History may also find the text valuable for their course studies.

Foreword by Prof. Rekha Saxena, Head, Department of Political Science, University of Delhi

THE AUTHORS

SHUBHRA PARMAR, Ph.D., Assistant Professor, Department of Political Science, Bhagini Nivedita College, University of Delhi. She has 12 years of teaching experience at University of Delhi and has written three academic books.

TANNI MOITRA, Ph.D. & Postdoc in History, Assistant Professor of History, School of Humanities & Social Sciences, Sharda University, Greater Noida.

ISBN:978-93-5443-927-8

9 789354 439278

₹ 475.00

www.phindia.com